A Practical Guide To Performance Appraisals

Karen Gendron, DVM

Copyright © 2002 by American Animal Hospital Association

press

12575 W. Bayaud Ave.
Lakewood, CO 80228
800/252-2242
press.aahanet.org

All rights reserved. No part of this publication may be reproduced or transmitted in any form or by any means, electronic or mechanical, including photocopying, without written permission of the American Animal Hospital Association.

Cataloging-in-Publication Data is available from the Library of Congress

ISBN 978-1-58326-033-3

CONTENTS

HOW TO USE THIS BOOK 1
    An Explanation of the Icons 2

CHAPTER 1: BENEFITS OF THE REVIEW 3
    Improve Employee Performance 4
    Strengthen Employee Commitment to Your Practice 5
    Encourage Pursuit of Mutual Goals 6
    Summary 10

CHAPTER 2: TIMING OF REVIEWS 11
    New Employees 12
    Established Employees 18
    Special Reviews 20
    Summary 22

CHAPTER 3: CHOOSING THE RIGHT KIND OF REVIEW 23
    Traditional Reviews 24
    World Reviews 25
    Summary 29

CHAPTER 4: PREPARING FOR THE REVIEW 31
    Employee Preparation 31
    Information Gathering 33
    Collecting Your Thoughts 35
    Building a Useful Evaluation 36
    Summary 38

CHAPTER 5: AVOIDING POTENTIAL PITFALLS 39
    Errors 39
    Eliminating Errors in the World Review 43
    Summary 45

CHAPTER 6: **COMPLETING THE TRADITIONAL REVIEW FORM**..................47
    Performance Criteria..48
    Overall Performance..65
    Summary...70

CHAPTER 7: **COMPLETING THE WORLD REVIEW FORM**............................71
    Variations on Standards for the World Review.........................72
    Numerical Rating Scale..74
    Explanation of Specific Areas for Evaluation 76
    Performance Criteria..77
    Evaluating Veterinarians and Managers...................................84
    Asking for Comments 87
    Tallying the Results 88
    Summarizing the Results 92
    Summary...95

CHAPTER 8: **GOAL SETTING** 97
    Goals to Correct Deficiencies 98
    Goals for the Practice 98
    Personal Goals 99
    Summary...100

CHAPTER 9: **THE REVIEW MEETING** 101
    Preliminaries 101
    The Ratings..103
    Performance Problems 105
    General Tips 107
    Goal Setting...111
    Summarize the Review 113
    Barriers to Effective Communication....................................113
    Salary Changes 118
    Evaluating the Evaluation..120
    Summary...121

CHAPTER 10: **DISCIPLINARY ACTION AND LEGAL ISSUES** 123
    The Performance Appraisal as a Legal Document 124
    Policies and Procedures 125
    Employment-at-Will 126
    Disciplinary Action 131
    Appeals and Arbitration 139
    Dismissal 141
    Summary 144

APPENDIX 1: **SAMPLE EMPLOYEE HANDBOOK SECTION ON EMPLOYEE APPRAISALS** 145

APPENDIX 2: **SOFTWARE PROGRAMS** 147

APPENDIX 3: **FORMS** 149
    World Evaluation Form 151
    Completed World Evaluation Form 154
    Traditional Evaluation Form 160
    Completed Traditional Evaluation Form 162
    Formal Commendation 164
    Completed Formal Commendation 165
    Formal Warning 166
    Completed Formal Warning 167

REFERENCES 169

INDEX 171

LIST OF TABLES

TABLE 2-1
    Suggested Goals for New Hires 14

TABLE 3-1
    Time Cost of a Traditional Review
    Versus a World Review 28

TABLE 4-1
    Skills to Emphasize (by position) 37

TABLE 7-1
    Summarizing the Results 90

TABLE 10-1
    Recommended Communication Procedures 139

ACKNOWLEDGEMENTS

Thank you to my family for your love and support. Your faith strengthens me. Thanks especially to my husband, Robert, and to my daughter, Lauren, who slept just enough nights for me to finish this book. Thanks to my parents, Earl and Blanche Clifford, who willingly vetted the legal chapter.

How To Use This Book

Once or twice a year, you should evaluate the performance of your employees. Yet you may have never studied human resource management or learned how to perform an effective evaluation and thus find the process challenging. As if you don't have enough to do to already, performance appraisals require you to focus your energy on paperwork and time-consuming individual meetings. The worst part is that you do not necessarily effect positive change with the review, despite having expended all that time and energy.

The good news is, it doesn't have to be that way. This book will walk you through the process of

- deciding when to perform reviews (Chapter 2),
- deciding which type of review is most appropriate (Chapter 3),
- preparing for the review (Chapter 4), and
- ensuring that you and your employees truly benefit from the process (Chapters 5-9).

This book is a step-by-step guide through the review process. It will help you through the decisions you need to make and point out some potential pitfalls.

A PRACTICAL GUIDE TO PERFORMANCE APPRAISALS

Every veterinarian and staff member should read the accompanying employee booklet. It details what your employees should expect from the review process and how they can prepare for their own reviews.

AN EXPLANATION OF THE ICONS

Special icons are used throughout this guide to emphasize concepts and points that are especially important for you to consider.

 Vital information you need to conduct any performance appraisal.

 Firsthand knowledge provided by the author, based on her own experience, to enhance your understanding of a concept or situation.

 Recommendations for a specific course of action that will give you the best possible results in the review process.

 Specific, helpful ideas that will allow you to make informed, wise decisions regarding the performance appraisal process.

 A special advisory regarding problems you may encounter during the review process.

CHAPTER 1

BENEFITS OF THE REVIEW

Sweaty palms and a churning stomach. Is this you when it is time for employee evaluations? A little anxiety is to be expected, because a poorly performed review can take months to correct. One study by Longenecker and Gioia in the summer 1988 *Sloan Management Review* suggested that effective reviews occur only 20 percent of the time for staff and even less frequently for managers. Fortunately, with a little preparation, you can provide outstanding reviews that will improve communication, motivation, growth, and productivity.

Most people think of reviews as constructive (or not-so-constructive) criticism. Employees think that their days of good, hard work will be ignored in favor of the moments when their performance could be improved. What *should* be the most rewarding and affirming time for employer and employee instead becomes the most stressful. You know that you're supposed to give reviews, but you don't want to risk a negative experience.

Employee reviews are *not* something you should do because your lawyer tells you to or just because they are part of your salary-review process. You conduct performance reviews because, done properly, they will

- improve employee performance,
- strengthen employee commitment to your practice, and
- encourage pursuit of mutual goals.

IMPROVE EMPLOYEE PERFORMANCE

What gets rewarded gets done. Your employees will want to repeat performance they are praised for. To ensure repetition of desired behaviors, you need to let employees know what those behaviors are. Most employees want fair and unbiased feedback. Those who don't want your feedback need it anyway. Although there are moments every day when you can provide this feedback, the review gives you a broad opportunity to recognize and reward the times when your employees succeeded in achieving their work-related goals. This lets them know where they meet your expectations and encourages them to continue this success.

One-fourth of veterinary staff members list poor communication as their biggest reason for job dissatisfaction in an October/November 1998 *Firstline* reader survey. Don't let that be the complaint at your hospital.

By communicating openly and fairly during the review, you are encouraging an environment that promotes open communication between you and your employees on all job-related issues. This pays off every day you work. You are setting the stage for an ongoing discussion with your employees regarding their work, and employees recognize that you deal with problems. For example, if you let your receptionist know during her review that you are willing to role-play difficult client situations with her, she will discuss with you interactions she finds troublesome. This kind of discussion will, in turn, help that employee improve her performance and make her feel like she is an important team member in your practice.

The review also formally documents each employee's work performance and future goals. You will discuss areas where your employee needs to improve and, with the employee, chart a course to achieve that improvement. Your employee has a right to know where her performance stands in relation to *acceptable* performance and *ideal* job performance. If she understands this at the end of the review and invests herself in the goals that you and she agreed on, you are guaranteed enhanced employee performance in the coming year.

The review is an opportunity to give positive feedback *and* to redirect your employees, which will boost employee performance. If an employee has a rough spot, she can improve her performance if you specifically identify the problem and work with her toward a solution. Part of your review, then, might include, "Mary, I think there is still room for improvement with your phone skills. When you are busy at the front desk, you can sometimes come across as abrupt to the caller." From there, you can develop a plan of action to enhance performance in that specific area.

Enhance performance through open, honest communication and directed goals. Increased employee performance will translate to higher productivity, greater income and profitability, higher wages, and, hopefully, fewer headaches for you.

STRENGTHEN EMPLOYEE COMMITMENT TO YOUR PRACTICE

If the review is effective, it will help to create a pleasant, productive work environment for your employees. This, in turn, strengthens your employees' commitment to your practice. Over time, the problems become fewer and farther between. Your staff works better as a unit and is able to eliminate inefficiencies. Who wouldn't want to keep working in that environment?

When your review includes your plans for the organization and explains how the employee is an integral part of achieving the plan, the employee becomes a stronger team member. She knows she is contributing in a more comprehensive fashion than she might at first realize. Even a kennel assistant is an integral part of reaching the goals of your practice, and she should know this. Such knowledge enhances each employee's self-worth, as well as her commitment to your practice. This employee is happier to come to work and contributes to a better working environment.

Your employees will be disappointed if, during the review, they do not sense commitment from you and a bond with your practice. As nervous as they are about sitting down with you, your employees want a fair review and an opportunity to talk to you about their role in your business. The review is their greatest opportunity for receiving your undivided attention. You are focusing solely on their achievements and avenues for professional growth, and you are identifying their individual roles in your vision for your practice. Their commitment means lower employee turnover, resulting in cost savings and fewer breaks in productivity.

ENCOURAGE PURSUIT OF MUTUAL GOALS

Did you know that your receptionist is taking night classes in accounting? That your associate veterinarian wants to build an "exotic" animal clientele? That your office manager wants to start a family and would still like to work if she can get more flexible hours? That your technician has been reading a lot about dentistry and thinks she can help you expand that part of your practice? Does your staff know that you are going to a four-day hands-on seminar on ultrasound because you are planning to add ultrasound services to your practice this year?

Goals are a two-way street. You can tell your staff what your goals are for the practice until you are blue in the face, but if they don't understand their part in achieving those goals, or if they do not agree with them, you will not accomplish them. Likewise, you need to be aware of your staff's goals for their careers and, sometimes, for their personal lives.

Each employee needs to know how she fits into your organization and how her work affects your goals for your hospital. If your goal is to expand your services next year to include acupuncture or more in-house lab equipment, your veterinarians, technicians, and assistants must be part of that goal. They must have or gain the technical skills required to assist you. Your receptionists must have an understanding of the value of these procedures so that they will support your recommendations for services to your clientele. If your goal is to see four more clients per day, your receptionists and technicians need to increase your efficiency by booking the additional clients and taking on additional nonmedical tasks. In short, you need to apprise them of your intent to expand services, gain their support, and help them to develop the new skills they will need.

There is no better time than at the review to share your vision with an employee and to ask her to share her personal vision with you. As you help your staff meet their personal goals, your practice and your work environment will improve. Meeting an employee's goals of flexible scheduling will bond her to your practice. Allowing your technician to pursue continuing education in dentistry and upgrading your equipment will expand a profit center. Explaining to your employees how ultrasound will benefit your practice and how they will be involved in assisting or educating clients will give you the building blocks to attain your goals.

Discussing goals has other practical purposes. Goals are a way to track your employee's progress. Without goals, how will your employee know what to work on to improve job performance, and how will she know at the end of the year whether or not she met your expectations? Establish goals at the time an employee is hired and review them at regular intervals thereafter.

During the review, you will discuss which goals were met and which were exceeded. You will also discuss why some goals were not met. Was your employee not motivated to accomplish the task? Was she incapable of accomplishing it? Was sufficient training provided and a reasonable time period for success given? You must be specific about your expectations and goals for each employee so that you can credibly determine whether or not the employee is on track.

I had a groomer who wanted to learn to "hand strip" dogs to expand the services she was able to offer. We developed a plan for her to attain that skill and to grow a client base that wanted that particular service. By her next review, she had not taken any of the necessary steps to meet that goal and so had not met her, or my, expectations. In effect, the planning time had been wasted, and an opportunity for improving service had been lost, at least temporarily. In my eyes, the employee's potential had been diminished somewhat. However, because we had specifically discussed and agreed upon her development of this skill as a goal, I was able to track her progress and take appropriate action.

Another time I needed a receptionist to learn how to run reports that would track kennel occupancy off our computer database. She was willing to learn this new skill and followed the plan we had developed to meet this goal. This employee was on track, and I rewarded her for it.

Look not only at the individual goals set for each employee, but at the goals you set for your practice. Did your practice meet its goals? If your hospital's performance met your financial and service goals, it is because your employees were committed to helping you. This commitment comes from awareness of their role in meeting your goals and a desire to reach them.

SHARING GOALS WITH EMPLOYEES WHO DON'T SEEM TO CARE

I hear some of you thinking out loud about your practice. You may have some employees who don't seem to care, yet you keep them around because you can't get the employees you want with the applicant pool in your area. You think everything I just said is going to be a hard sell with these employees, because they don't appear to want to succeed in their jobs and certainly aren't invested in the practice.

Don't beat your head against the wall. Everything I just said about reviews is equally true for these employees. The biggest difference is that you are not entering the review assuming these employees want to do their jobs to the best of their ability. *You are going to have to work harder to give them an incentive to be good, productive employees.*

You can still use the review as a tool to record their performance and identify areas for improvement. Concentrate on reasons personal to them that might help them improve. It may mean figuring out what *is* important to these workers. For example, if money is important, give them a pay increase when they achieve their goals. If you can help them attain their individual goals—however unrelated to your practice—you will still bond them to your practice and encourage them to work harder toward *your* goals.

If your applicant pool improves, you can justify letting an unsatisfactory employee go. Make sure, however, that you don't give up on an employee too soon. A well-thought-out, quality review process may jump-start this employee.

I was in this position with two kennel workers who seemed to just be putting in the time. Unfortunately, my applicant pool was so small, not a single applicant made it past a screening phone call. Barring a major incident, I needed to keep these kennel workers in their jobs to provide whatever level of service possible. When a specific, identifiable problem arose with their performance, I noted it.

One kennel worker continued to show up late for work and couldn't seem to administer medications to kennel dogs on schedule. Despite additional training and two written warnings, I saw no improvement—or any interest in improvement. I ended up firing her but felt comfortable that my decision was justified and that I had the documentation to substantiate my position. Fortunately, I was able to talk the brother of a receptionist into working for a few weeks while he was conducting a job search so that the kennel staff situation didn't become more dire.

The other kennel worker listened carefully when I discussed a problem with her. She was willing to accept additional training and supervision. Slowly, but surely, she improved. Whenever her performance would slide back a bit, we would sit down again, but the meetings were constructive. She turned out to be a reliable and capable worker.

An employee who is not interested in your practice may remain so and may become a candidate for termination. A well-executed review will enable you to determine if the employee stands a chance of buying in and taking a crucial step toward investing in her job.

SUMMARY

Performance reviews are a critical practice-management tool. When appraisals are done effectively, they bond your team and improve individual performance, which ultimately improves your practice. However, if your review is ineffective, it may cause your employees to become even *less* motivated. The changes may come slowly and grudgingly at first as your staff adjusts to the review process, but in a couple of years, you will have a stellar team that works well together because they have been given the information and support they need to be successful in your practice.

CHAPTER 2

TIMING OF REVIEWS

Performance reviews are usually given annually. Many businesses use the employee's anniversary date as the review date. This allows you to spread out your evaluations and to address each employee in a consistent time frame. An employee hired in July isn't then being judged on five months worth of work in a December review, as opposed to the employee hired in February, who has almost a year's worth of accomplishments to show.

Other veterinary practices perform their reviews in December or January. These are typically slower months that allow you the time to spend on this process. If you offer a year-end bonus tied to performance, this is the only time of year it makes sense to perform reviews. (See pages 118–120 for a discussion on reviews and pay changes.)

However you schedule your reviews, what is most important is that reviews be done in a timely and consistent fashion. If you are performing a June review in November, you have minimized the importance of the process and degraded your employee's motivation.

FOR BEST RESULTS

It is important to ensure that all your staff members are treated equitably in the process. When all your reviews are performed at one time of year, complete them within two weeks—no matter how large your staff. Imagine how unimportant an employee feels when she is reviewed four weeks after other employees because you couldn't fit her into your schedule sooner.

TIP

Follow up these annual reviews with a six-month progress check. If that seems too laborious, set up an alternate system to keep track of an employee's postreview progress. One alternative is to keep a calendar marked with the dates on which employees are to achieve each goal, then continuously monitor whether or not your employees are on course.

NEW EMPLOYEES

New employees need direction as soon as they walk through the door. They need to know who is responsible for training them and who will answer their questions. They also should know what you expect them to learn and accomplish over the next few months and what will happen if they do not meet your expectations.

FOR BEST RESULTS

New employees can quickly get off-track. For the uninitiated, work in a veterinary hospital is hectic and overwhelming—there is so much to learn. Constant communication during this early time is critical to ensure that new employees will be productive and happy. Those first days on the job can set the tone for how an employee subsequently performs; therefore, you need to maintain a positive attitude. A well-constructed start will reduce problems stemming from misunderstandings about the practice's operations or policies.

DAY ONE

On the day the employee is hired, or the day she starts work, provide her with a copy of your review form. From this, your new hire will be shown what you expect of her and how she will be evaluated. Set goals you expect your new employee to accomplish during her first week and during her trial period—typically three months (see Table 2-1). Then talk about your plan to help her meet these goals. For some goals, like showing up on time and being ready to work, she is on her own. For other objectives, like learning to invoice clients on your computer system, tell her who will be training her and how long it should take before she is comfortable performing this task on her own. Without spending your entire day going into the minute details of her job, be as specific as you can. The more specific you are about skills the new employee is expected to develop and within what time period, the less confusion there will be. You won't end up with your new hire telling you at the end of the first week that she did not understand she was supposed to know how to schedule an appointment by now.

This process is equally important for your recently hired associate veterinarians. They also need a clear idea of your expectations and who they can seek out for answers.

Week One

I recommend an informal meeting with your new hire at the end of her first week. The person performing the review can be the practice owner, the manager, or the employee's direct supervisor.

At this time, it is nice to sit down with a cup of coffee and find out how your new employee's week has been. Does she feel held back—that she's ready for additional training and responsibilities? Does she feel overwhelmed or that she is not getting the training support she needs? This is your opportunity to nip problems in the bud. *You do not want to wait to discuss pertinent issues until the end of a three-month trial period, when problems may have progressed so far it will be difficult to correct them.*

TABLE 2-1

SUGGESTED GOALS FOR NEW HIRES[1]

VETERINARIAN

One week: Is capable of performing standard medical and surgical procedures

One month: Is familiar with any practice equipment or medications previously unfamiliar with

Is ready to develop own clientele

Three months: Has full knowledge of hospital policies and procedures

TECHNICIAN

One week: Is able to vaccinate and medicate

Is able to properly restrain patients

One month: Is able to answer client questions and provide patient updates

Is able to dispense medications

Has adequate medical record keeping skills

Is able to perform routine dental procedures

Has surgical capability (induction, preparation, monitoring, and instrument care)

Is familiar with hospital equipment

Is able to take and develop radiographs

Three months: Has knowledge of hospital policies and procedures

Is able to do inventory control and ordering

Is able to restock

Is able to handle certain types of client visits along (such as suture removals, bandage changes, introductory vaccine boosters)

[1] The job requirements for each title vary tremendously among veterinary practices. For this reason, each practice should modify this chart to best suit its requirements.

TABLE 2-1 (cont'd)
SUGGESTED GOALS FOR NEW HIRES

RECEPTIONIST

One week:	Is able to file
	Is able to invoice
	Is able to check clients in
One month:	Is able to answer the phone effectively
	Can schedule appointments and surgery
	Has basic computer skills, including input of new information; updating client information; printing consent forms, estimates, and rabies certificates; and printing daily reports
	Can dispense medications
Three months:	Can answer commonly asked questions
	Has knowledge of hospital policies and procedures
	Has knowledge of over-the-counter products, including food, flea, and tick products

KENNEL ASSISTANT

One week:	Is able to properly and thoroughly clean and sanitize kennel runs
One month:	Is able to properly restrain animals
	Is able to medicate kenneled animals
Three months:	Is familiar with side effects of medications taken by kenneled animals
	Is able to report potential health problems of kenneled animals

A PRACTICAL GUIDE TO PERFORMANCE APPRAISALS

Take this opportunity to focus your new employee's attention on the next few months. Reemphasize or reset goals. Again, discuss a game plan for reaching these goals. If there is a significant problem—for example, your new hire has been late for work two out of the five days she has been scheduled—issue a reprimand. Let her know what the consequences will be if she is late again. Every employee deserves fair warning.

This informal sit-down is also an ideal chance to get your new employee's perspective. People who haven't been working with your system for years bring original ideas and question why things are done a certain way. You may have very good reasons why things are done a particular way in your hospital, but before you say that to your new employee, listen to any thoughts, questions, and suggestions she has. While you are listening, take notes. This will show her that you value her thoughts and are considering them. If you interrupt with reasoning, she will be reluctant to continue. When she has given you her thoughts thank her and tell her you hope she will continue to bring up these issues. Then you may explain if there is a valid reason for doing things the way you do. If the reason is habit, it might be time to let the staff decide if there is a better, more efficient way to accomplish the task.

Month One

Your new hire has survived the first month. She hasn't blown up the computer, alienated your best client, or sent a client home with the wrong cat. She might be a keeper. Therefore, you need to sit down with her for her first real review. This appraisal can be less detailed than the annual review. At this point, however, you have something concrete to talk to her about. Let her know how she is fitting into the organization and whether she has met the goals you set for her during her first month. Identify any roadblocks in her training program and decide how to bypass them.

16

Ask again for suggestions on ways in which the hospital could improve its services.

If your new employee is seriously behind in her training at this point, you must consider whether she can catch up and be productive in a reasonable period of time. Have there been any major problems? Has she been rude to a client, uncooperative with a coworker, or given out incorrect information to clients? Use this meeting to identify problems and to ensure they will be corrected. Let her know what the consequences will be if any of these problem behaviors continue.

This is also your opportunity to outline for your employee what you expect of her over the next couple of months. Her new goals will include new skills as well as corrections of any problems you have identified.

If your new employee has exhibited serious problem behaviors or does not appear to have the aptitude for this work by the end of the first month, it is best to let her go now. Although you have already invested a significant amount of time into this employee and may be tempted to keep going, don't. If it is truly clear that this employee will not work out, you are losing time and would be better off hiring an employee who will have a better chance of meeting your standards. Continuing to permit substandard performance and conflict will demoralize your staff. Some people simply need more time and can become fabulous employees if they are allowed to move at their own pace. It is a huge gamble to invest another six months in an employee just to find that out.

Month Three

Three months is, traditionally, the end of the trial period for new employees. You must formally decide to keep the employee or let her go.

If your new employee is just not understanding her job fully, if she is causing staff conflict, or if you have not seen improvement in undesirable work behaviors that you have discussed, tell her that you are not continuing her employment. Do not compromise the potential of your practice. Do not lead your staff to believe that this level of performance is acceptable in your practice. Let this person go so that she can find a position at which she can succeed.

If you are experiencing problems with your new hire that you believe can still be worked out, consider extending the trial period. You can't extend the trial period indefinitely, but another month might give you the time you need. This will put your employee on notice that there is very little time to correct a performance problem.

Hopefully, you will not be in either of these situations. Instead, you will find that your new employee is learning quickly, getting along well with her teammates, and bonding with your clients and their pets. Let her know, with some excitement, that she has completed her trial period and is now a full-fledged member of your proud staff. Set goals for the period until her annual review and clarify any remaining issues regarding her duties. For example, if a new kennel assistant has not yet given insulin (or other) injections, let her know precisely when you expect her to be comfortable performing this task. Be very specific about any significant areas on which you want her to work.

ESTABLISHING EMPLOYEES

In an ideal world, you would offer some level of review to employees at least every month. But that is just not practical, is it? You certainly should give your employees constant feedback regarding their performance. Have you let today pass without telling your receptionist how well she handled that difficult client? Have you advised your kennel person that the hour-and-a-half

TIMING OF REVIEWS

lunch she took today was not appropriate? Have you given kudos to your veterinarian for successfully managing a challenging case? Those are not issues that should wait for the annual review.

In the hectic world of the average veterinary practice, it can seem a Herculean task to make the time for annual reviews, let alone consider more frequent reviews. If you could sit down with your employees every six months, it would take more time and cost more to administer the reviews. You would, however, be able to provide more accurate and timely feedback. You would have greater opportunity to keep your staff on track and follow the goals you have set.

Which goal do you think you will meet faster—the one that is a passing thought every few months, or the one you see in front of you every day? Naturally, the more focused you are on achieving your goals, the more likely you are to meet them. How long do you want to wait before you correct performance problems or reward employees for work well done? The more frequent the feedback, the better you can fine-tune job performance. There is a limit, though, to the fine-tuning. Full-fledged reviews more often than twice a year are not likely to have any significant impact on behavior modification.

If you can manage reviews every six months, you should do them. If you cannot, be sure to provide feedback at least once a year and pay close attention to the potential errors listed in Chapter Five. The likelihood of errors occurring increases with a longer interval between evaluations.

The advantage of conducting reviews every six months instead of yearly is that you are able to evaluate and reset goals frequently. You can respond quickly to changes in your work climate, such as new employees or a change in the business plan. You can give your employees the opportunity for more frequent rewards and for earlier warnings if there are performance problems.

Some businesses find a middle ground by performing a full, formal evaluation once a year and doing a progress check at the six-month mark. An alternative might be to keep a calendar marked with all the dates by which goals should be met. If an employee's goal is to produce the spring hospital newsletter by March 1, that date is marked on your calendar with a notation. On March 1, you then check to see if the goal has been met. If it has been achieved, congratulate your employee. If it has not been met, talk to the employee so that she can get back on track and recommit to the goal.

SPECIAL REVIEWS

Not all problems coincide with the timing of your annual reviews, and some problems are too big to address in an informal way. Whenever you have a serious problem with an employee, you need to sit down with her and document the problem. Special review sessions (as opposed to strictly disciplinary action) should be held when

- an employee brings personal problems to work, significantly impacting the staff or practice;
- an employee is causing trouble, such as gossiping, blaming others for her errors, arguing with fellow employees, or speaking badly of the hospital or staff to clients; or
- an employee's work is so substandard you cannot wait for the regular review.

Let's say your receptionist, Andrea, is divorcing her husband of ten years and is fighting for custody of her two children. She seems to be spending work time every day talking to her lawyer and fighting with her husband. As if this weren't disruptive enough, she has some of these discussions on the phone at the front desk, where all the staff and clients in the room can hear her. As sympathetic as you are for her situation, you must set guidelines for this out-of-control situation. You may be able to give her fifteen minutes each day during which she will be permitted to make phone calls from your office. You must explain to her that she may no longer make or take personal calls while she is working, nor may she discuss her situation at work.

In another possible scenario, it's Tuesday night and you are stopping back at the hospital to check on a sick patient. You see Bill, your kennel assistant, place a large bag of dog food in his trunk and leave. He is the only one at the hospital this late. You check the day's billings and see that the food was not charged to his account, and there is no note to mention that he will be paying for the food the next day. Whether you determine that his intent was to steal the food or not, provide a review the next day. Terminate his employment or clarify the hospital's policy on employee purchases. Put the discussion in writing and have Bill sign the page. Be clear on what the consequences will be if there is another breach in policy.

Jill has always performed her duties as your technician satisfactory—until this week, that is. Jill started taking evening classes this year, and this is finals week. You suspect she's spending all her sleep time studying instead of sleeping. She seems distracted and tired. Fortunately, you caught her before she administered the wrong medication to a patient. Aside from that, she is really slowing down the surgery schedule. While you want to support Jill's efforts at continuing education, she can't let her studies interfere with her work. Patients may be at risk. Don't wait for finals to be over and hope that she catches up on her sleep. Sit down with her and let her know that she needs to manage her commitments better, because this level of work is unacceptable.

All unscheduled reviews shouldn't be for problems. Do you remember the feeling you get when your boss unexpectedly comes up to you and asks to see you in his office? Did you ever think it was something good he wanted to talk to you about? Let your employees know that you call them in for compliments and positive feedback as well.

For example, your kennel assistant, Jane, is walking through the kennel and sees a Doberman having dry heaves. She opens the kennel to comfort the dog and check on him and notices that his belly seems swollen. She interrupts the doctor so that the problem can be attended to immediately, ultimately allowing the bloat to be resolved successfully. In another instance, your technician, Sarah, goes to the local grade school to give a presentation in coordination with National Pet Week. She does a great job and is highlighted in the local newspaper for the effort.

Achievements such as these deserve special recognition and a formal commendation letter placed in the employee's file. If you prefer, you may use forms to guide your discussions. An example of a commendation is found on page 165. However, even with a formal commendation, be sure to tell your employee what you found so wonderful.

SUMMARY

One yearly review isn't sufficient for all employees. New employees, especially, need frequent evaluation and feedback. The goal-setting process should begin the day an employee is hired and should be continued on a frequent, regular basis. All employees can benefit by frequent feedback, but there is a higher cost associated with conducting reviews more than once a year. Whether you choose to conduct your reviews annually or biannually, keep in mind that events may occur that will trigger a special commendation or warning.

CHAPTER 3

Choosing the Right Kind of Review

There are almost as many ways to get through the review process as there are businesses. Some businesses do not conduct reviews at all. For others, the review process amounts to daily tidbits of feedback related to the task at hand. Some companies are evolving to "coaching" situations as opposed to traditional reviews. With management by objectives, employees develop the standards against which their performance is measured so that they are more motivated to achieve their goals. The supervisor and employee meet to develop challenging goals for the next period.

The latest wave in the performance appraisal is the world or multirater review. However, many companies still stick with the old-fashioned, traditional appraisal process where the manager is in charge. Even then, there are differences. Some evaluations use a 1-10 rating scale, others involve check-off columns, such as "meets job expectations," and others use essay-style answers to open-ended questions. Each business, and each practice, alters the process to fit its personality and philosophy.

In this chapter, you will learn about two common frameworks to consider as the basis for your reviews. There are many variations within each framework, including what standard of evaluation to use, how much data to gather, and how often you should conduct the review. The procedures and forms can be modified to best fit your practice, as long as you are sure the change does not negatively impact the two-way feedback and goals of the review.

TRADITIONAL REVIEWS

The traditional review has been used by American businesses for many years. In the traditional review, the employee's direct supervisor or manager is in charge. The reviewer fills out an evaluation form to assess the employee's performance and also conducts the review itself. The reviewer may gather information from other staff members or through the evaluation of objective data. This type of review is very effective when the manager has good and personal knowledge of the employee's performance, is free of bias, and has a good working relationship with the employee. Because the manager is also the evaluator, subjective parts of the evaluation are from the manager's point of view.

The advantage of a traditional review is that it is less costly and time consuming than a world review. The traditional review is best for small practices where there would be no more than two evaluators. (At least three evaluators are necessary for a proper world evaluation.) It is also appropriate for practices in which the owner or manager does not want input from the rest of the staff, whether for reasons of time or management philosophy. If you do not believe your staff is ready to fairly participate in the evaluation of other staff members, choose a traditional review.

WORLD REVIEWS

The second type of review I will call a "world review" for simplicity. The most common term used for this type of review is a "360-degree review," but it is also referred to as an "upward" or "multirater review." I prefer the term "world" because it expresses that the review comes from everyone in the employee's world. Although the world review takes more time, it is a better way to evaluate your employees as long as the information is credible.

The world review takes the input of many reviewers, providing a better view of the employee's work behaviors in a variety of work situations. A supervisor cannot possibly see everything. Between the supervisor, the coworkers, and the customers, however, you can paint a very detailed picture of performance. Employees also learn that they are accountable to all other staff members, because the entire staff gives feedback. This enhances a team focus and encourages employees to do their best job at all times.

There is greater credibility with a world review, because the appraisal cannot be overly influenced by a single person's perspective (presuming that the manager does not discount other reviewers). Properly done, world reviews have less risk of bias and other errors because of the multiple-source perspective and because responses can be evaluated for bias. Another tremendous advantage for the supervisor is that employees are less likely to discredit information that has come collectively from coworkers. According to studies by Edwards and Ewen, authors of 360° *Feedback*, employees perceive world feedback to be more fair than traditional, single-rater feedback.

I find that the greatest potential of the world review is at learning hospitals that promote a true team environment. In fact, if you call for teamwork and team thinking in your practice, yet conduct a traditional review, you are sending a mixed message to your staff. You send the message that your team is not capable of evaluating itself and that members cannot be trusted with the evaluation.

These evaluations are a natural step for practices that have empowered employees and an open management system. With the world review, the supervisor takes on the role of coach, not judge.

Although this discussion pertains to the world system for the purpose of evaluating your employee's performance, this feedback system is also used as a basis for rewards, to improve communication, and to obtain strategic data on which to base other initiatives. For example, the system might be used to identify employee strengths and weaknesses that may affect the success of a future project. Some companies use a world review strictly for career development. Sometimes, this use is the first step toward familiarizing employees with the world process, so that the evaluations can be used later for performance appraisals.

FOR BEST RESULTS

When choosing the world review, you first need to establish who the reviewers will be. The number of evaluators will depend on your environment. There should be at least three evaluators in addition to the supervisor and the employee (who will complete the self-evaluation). If you have a very large practice, six evaluators should be sufficient to gather the necessary perspective. It is unnecessary to have thirty evaluators. The evaluators for a kennel assistant who works only on Sunday when the hospital is closed may be limited to other kennel assistants and the direct supervisor, for example. The evaluators for a receptionist would include other receptionists, the doctors, the office manager, kennel assistants, and technicians—all of whom interact with the receptionist.

Although it isn't often done due to the difficulty of obtaining the information, an ideal world review includes brief evaluations by clients and vendors who come in contact with the employee. For example, your suppliers evaluate a technician or manager who handles inventory and ordering. Your doctors, receptionists, and office assistants can be evaluated by a select group of clients. All of these people directly impact your business.

A good employee deals effectively with all of these groups. Without this degree of evaluation, how can you know how well your employee handles her job? If your manager does not have a good relationship with your suppliers, there is a good chance she is not hearing about all the special deals or receiving quick responses. If your exam-room assistant is not rated highly by your clients in terms of knowledge, you know you need to set some continuing education and communication goals for her.

TIME COST OF THE WORLD REVIEW

So, why wouldn't everyone want to perform a world review? Well, the bad news is that world reviews are very time consuming. Your staff will need to be trained to perform evaluations, and you will need to allow time for the employees to do their reviews and collate the information. This adds to the cost of performing a review.

Consider the example of a practice with a staff of ten performing a traditional versus a world review. Table 3.1 depicts the evaluation to highlight steps that require a significant difference in outlay of time. Although many aspects of the review process, including the time to design the review form, print the forms, and conduct the review, are equivalent for the traditional and world reviews, there are two areas in which the world review demands substantially more time. With the traditional review, a training session for supervisors might take two hours; the time to complete the forms, at an estimated thirty minutes per form, is five hours; and no time is needed to compile the data from different forms. With the world review, you might double your training time because you now need a training session for the employees as well as for the supervisors. The time it takes for all employees to complete their forms adds up to forty-five hours, and another five hours are required to compile the data. The difference in time is 47 hours, based on a staff of ten.

You must feel very comfortable with this review process yourself so that you can train your staff in how to complete a world evaluation form. For staff members who have never been managers

TABLE 3-1
TIME COST OF A TRADITIONAL VERSUS A WORLD REVIEW

	Traditional Review	World Review
Design Form	++	++
Print Form	+	+
Distribute Form	+	+
Design Process	++	+++
Train Managers How to Conduct Appraisal	+	++
Fill Out Forms	+	++++
Compile Evaluations	N/A	++++
Set Goals	+	+
Conduct Review	+	+
Handle Appeals and Grievances	?	? In theory, fewer

or evaluators, this is a big step requiring a significant amount of support. Staff training should include reading the pamphlet that accompanies this book and attending an in-house seminar on evaluations. Staff members need to understand the criteria you use in evaluating an employee fully and must be prepared to provide honest and thorough feedback. Employees should also be given a contact person who can answer their questions or help them with problems. It is important that you plan the details of the training thoroughly and ensure that all staff members are up to the task.

If you have not created an open, healthy work environment, your staff may not provide honest evaluations. Instead, they may take the opportunity to belittle other staff members if they believe it will enhance their position. Thankfully, there are ways to avoid that pitfall by insisting on a thorough and specific evaluation. (See Chapter Five for a full discussion of pitfalls.)

SUMMARY

The evaluation framework you choose should reflect the practice's environment and your management philosophy. A traditional evaluation is best for a small practice, whereas a world evaluation is best for a larger, team-based practice. Although there are a number of benefits to a world review, including less bias and greater credibility, there is also a downside in the training and amount of time the world review requires.

CHAPTER 4

PREPARING FOR THE REVIEW

EMPLOYEE PREPARATION

Your staff members need time to prepare for their reviews. Two weeks in advance of the review, let each staff member know the date of her evaluation. At that time, give her a copy of the review form you will be using and any guidelines you wish to provide. The pamphlet accompanying this book can be given to your employees to prepare them. Samples of review forms are found on pages 151–163. The only preparation required for a traditional review is that the employee must complete her self-evaluation form prior to the review.

Preparing for a world review requires more planning. Follow these steps for a world review:
- Provide instructions for completing the forms. It is important that employees use specific examples (although the manager will read all the examples, examples that identify the reviewer should not be used during the review itself in order to maintain anonymity).

- Make a packet of review forms for each employee. Write one name—that of the employee being evaluated—on top of each form, and give each employee her group of forms; i.e., one employee gets an evaluation form for every employee whom she is qualified to review.
- Tell your employees not to write their names or otherwise identify themselves on the evaluation.
- Give a deadline for returning all the evaluations.
- Tell your employees the person to whom they should return the forms.
- Poll vendors and clients, if possible, or give them a copy of the review form to return. Any outside sources used in an evaluation must have a working relationship with the employee and knowledge of that employee's work habits. The source may be questioned informally or given a review form to complete. An accountant may comment on your business manager. A sales representative might review your inventory manager. Clients might be appropriate evaluators for any employee who has client contact.

  As with in-house evaluators, three clients known to have contact with the employee would be a fair sampling. The trick is to choose the evaluators without bias (for example, choosing only good clients or clients known to have certain experience with the staff member). Certainly, an effective way to get appropriate feedback for your practice's employees is to regularly poll a random sample of clients to determine their experience with the practice and with specific staff members. A reasonable alternative might be to hand out the evaluation to randomly selected clients as they leave the practice following an appointment or procedure. They can be asked to evaluate one employee with whom you know they had contact that day.
- Have the employee fill out her self-evaluation.

INFORMATION GATHERING

FROM EMPLOYEES

Your primary source of information will be the review forms completed by the supervisor or office manager for a traditional review, or completed by a group of employees for a world review.

One of the faults of most review systems is that the feedback is likely to reflect the most recent history. For example, say that you typically perform reviews in December. Are you really going to remember that Sally showed up late twice last January and that she had a tiff with Jessica in June? The review is likely to more heavily reflect events over the most recent couple of months. This is called the error of recency. (See Chapter Five for a more complete discussion of this problem.)

To avoid that pitfall, keep notes throughout the year. In addition to conducting formal meetings or giving warnings, keep a record of everyday performance. Once a week, you can jot down some notes about your employees' performance that week. Give yourself short, specific examples of behavior.

If you are doing world reviews you can also space the information-gathering evaluations throughout the year for more accurate assessments. If you have ten employees who will all be rating each other, you can give each employee a month to complete her evaluations of others. In other words, one employee will do all her ratings in January, the second employee will do all her evaluations in February, and so on. In that way, you will have some perspective and specific examples of performance throughout the year. This method will not be as effective if you suffer from high employee turnover.

It is important to emphasize the need for specific examples. Many errors, including false scores from personal vendettas, will be avoided if evaluators must back up their ratings.

From Computer and Paper Records

Computerization has brought many benefits to veterinary practices, including the ability to summarize performance data quickly. Many hospitals already track a doctor's production and use IDs in their computer for other employees.

Have you considered using this information to help evaluate the performance of your nondoctor employees? For example, if all your employees must type in their ID to invoice a client, your database may allow you to sort total number of invoices by ID. You can then compare how many invoices each employee entered per month. It is a small piece of the puzzle in evaluating productivity, but an objective one. Do you have your receptionists initial the appointments they made in your appointment book? If you do, glance through a few months and see whose initials are there the most. That's the receptionist who is answering the phone most often and is perhaps the most effective at convincing callers to schedule the appointment.

There are many places where technicians' names are attached to their work, such as surgical and radiographic logs. Are you sure that all your technicians are sharing radiographic duty equally? Check your log. Maybe you will find a superstar who jumps in and completes radiographs quickly, on the first attempt. Or perhaps you'll find that one of your technicians often requires additional attempts or simply avoids taking radiographs.

When evaluating these numbers, always keep in mind adjusting for the number of hours each employee works. For technicians, especially, you may also have to account for differences based on shift demands.

In your practice, look at methods such as these to utilize information that is already available. Tracking this information will provide an objective means to evaluate productivity, and you want your evaluations to be as objective as possible.

There many be areas where you can predict an employee's productivity and later judge whether she met that estimate. Your receptionist or office manager might be asked, as part of her duties, to send out monthly vaccine and service reminders. Each month, she writes down the day the reminders were sent along with the number sent. If, therefore, your system is to send out reminders on the fifteenth of the month and you find that 25 percent of the time reminders are sent after the twentieth, that information can be used to assess an employee's timeliness and productivity. Perhaps your hospital schedules tech appointments. Does your stay on schedule with her appointments? Had you planned on four per hour but find that she is being scheduled for three so that she doesn't get behind? These are objective ways to evaluate an employee's level of productivity.

COLLECTING YOUR THOUGHTS

This is an especially good thing to do during your evening commute. Before you fill out the review form, begin to piece together in your mind answers to the following questions.

- What goals were set for this employee?
- Were these goals met?
- What are your goals for the practice?
- How can this employee help meet these goals?
- What are three specific examples of this employee's best performance?
- What are specific examples of this employee's worst performance?
- What are your goals for this employee for the next period?
- (Goals and goal setting are discussed more thoroughly in Chapter Eight.)

Once you have all that straight in your mind, you are ready to complete your review form.

A PRACTICAL GUIDE TO PERFORMANCE APPRAISALS

BUILDING A USEFUL EVALUATION

It is now time to take all your thoughts and the data you have collected and build a useful evaluation. Using a standard form will help frame your thoughts and lead you to constructive conclusions. You can use one of the forms included in this book (see Appendix 3) or design your own. If you choose to design your own to best meet the needs of your practice, remember that your goal is to define, measure, and evaluate the factors needed to sustain individual, team, and organizational effectiveness. One of the advantages of designing your own form is that your employees will accept the process better if they have some input in its setup.

There are two specific additions you may choose to make to these standard forms. On the world-review form, there is not a place for an evaluator's name. This is done purposely to ensure anonymity of responses. If, after reading this chapter, you believe it is important to know which evaluator gave which responses, be sure to add a place for the name. You may also find it helpful to assign importance scales to the evaluation categories. You can intuitively discern which skills are most important for different positions and highlight them. By highlighting the most relevant areas, you can focus the employee on critical areas and decide which areas are most valuable for development (see Table 4.1).

The review forms included in this book can be used for all employees: managers, doctors, receptionists, technicians, assistants, and groomers. There is no employee for whom these forms would be inappropriate.

Having said that, a more detailed evaluation will be needed for managers and veterinarians than these review forms allow for. A successful doctor will achieve high marks for all the attributes evaluated with the standard review form. These attributes contribute significantly to the doctor's value to your practice in terms of the doctor's ability to relate to clients and staff and to be an

TABLE 4-1
SKILLS TO EMPHASIZE
(BY POSITION)

Veterinarian
Attitude
Client Interaction
Communication Skills
Knowledge Base
Professional Appearance
Technical Skills

Manager
Attitude
Client Interaction
Communication Skills

Technician
Animal Handling
Knowledge Base
Organization/Cleanliness
Technical Skills

Receptionist
Attitude
Client Interaction
Communication Skills
Professional Appearance

Veterinary Assistant
Animal Handling
Technical Skills

Kennel Assistant
Animal Handling
Organization/Cleanliness

Groomer
Animal Handling
Technical Skills

All Positions
Productivity
Punctuality

effective service provider. However, doctors must also be evaluated on their medical and surgical abilities beyond the skills outlined in the basic review.

The review for a manager will similarly be based on the standard evaluation form. In addition, a thorough review of a manager includes evaluation of leadership ability, personnel management skills, financial management capabilities, and any specific management skill required for your practice. For example, while all employees are rated on communication skills, your manager will be evaluated specifically from the viewpoint of her communications skills while handling management issues (i.e., employee reprimands and past-due account collections).

SUMMARY

With both the traditional and world reviews, it is important to be thorough in your preparation and to take subjectivity out of the process wherever possible. This can be accomplished through record keeping and evaluation of objective data.

As you prepare for a review, be sure to give your employee two weeks for completing any self-evaluation forms, and give yourself time to collect your own thoughts. As soon as you have completed these steps, you need to develop useful evaluation forms that will work for your practice. Sample review forms are provided on pages 151–167.

CHAPTER 5

AVOIDING POTENTIAL PITFALLS

ERRORS

Many of the errors made during evaluations can be avoided by using objective, rather than subjective, criteria. Objective criteria are inherently unbiased. Subjectively, for example, you may presume that an employee has a good attendance record. Objectively, a time card review shows that same employee has been late eight days in the last two months. Subjectively, one technician may appear busier and thus more productive, yet an objective count of completed procedures shows this technician completes fewer procedures in a day than your other technicians. The world review process also eliminates many biases and errors because of the multiple sources from which information is gathered. Any bias by one evaluator is likely to be softened or eliminated when that evaluator's rating is considered against others.

ERROR OF RECENCY

It is always difficult to remember specific events that occurred several months earlier; therefore, reviews often reflect the most recent events. Employees may also improve their performance in preparation for their reviews. As a result, you may be inclined to give them a more positive appraisal, dismissing earlier performance. The error of recency is one reason why you should make salary changes separate from the performance review.

To avoid the recency error, use objective data collected over the entire evaluation period. True, objective facts do not lie. Keep notes throughout the evaluation period. This will jog your memory of more distant events. If you use a world-review process, have employees complete evaluations at different times so that you will have a series of snapshots over time when you conduct a review. If one evaluator fills out an evaluation for an employee in February, another completes an evaluation in April, and others give their evaluations in August and November, the error of recency becomes minimized. Each evaluator may still focus on a recent period, but different periods throughout the year are still being considered.

HALO EFFECT

An employee who is a superstar in one area may be rated highly in all categories even though she is not superior in all areas. Conversely, an employee who has remarkably poor performance in an area may receive substandard ratings in other areas as well. To avoid the halo effect, demand specific examples of performance. When specific examples back up statements of performance, you should get a more realistic picture. Insisting on examples for both poor and stellar performance helps eliminate the halo effect.

BIAS

The reviewer's prejudices and values will distort ratings if they are not held in check. The more you use objective criteria, the less bias will come into play. If a technician thinks that all receptionists are inherently ignorant about technical and medical matters, she will rate all receptionists poorly in any knowledge or technical-skill areas. If the technician is forced to consider specific examples in which each receptionist was capable or lacking, her bias alone would not determine the rating she gave every receptionist.

Self-bias also exists. Some people think themselves giants. In 360° *Feedback*, authors Edwards and Ewen point out that women and minorities tend to rate themselves lower than other evaluators would. All others tend to rate themselves higher. It is important that self-bias be recognized by the supervisor conducting a review so that a self-evaluation can be used correctly in the appraisal process.

CENTRAL TENDENCY

Some reviewers will rate all employees within a narrow range regardless of performance. This reviewer can be helped by clearly defining the standards for each point to be evaluated and by providing objective data. As an example, let's say you track client satisfaction. One receptionist gets an "excellent" rating from 90 percent of your clients, while another receives top ratings from only 70 percent of your clients. This reviewer might use that information to give the first receptionist a higher rating. If you break down skill levels for each position in your practice, this reviewer will be better able to judge which employees have actually reached higher skill levels.

STRICTNESS OR LENIENCY

Some appraisers will not give low scores because they don't want to hurt anyone. Other appraisers feel that the standards of

FOR BEST RESULTS

the business or of the employees are too low and therefore will rate everyone poorly. The strict and the lenient appraisers can be aided by having them use as much objective criteria as possible and by providing clear detail about the standard of performance for each job. When the strict appraiser must compare performance against the job standard alone, the appraiser must admit where an employee meets and exceeds the requirements of the job. A lenient appraiser's opinion could easily be altered by objective data. If a technician is expected to do a certain number of dentals but completes less than that number, the appraiser could not rate the technician highly in that specific category.

CONTRAST

The contrast error occurs when appraisers compare and contrast employees to each other and not to the objective performance standards set for the position. I am not sure that this tendency can be avoided completely. Training reviewers to use job requirements rather than comparative behaviors as a frame of reference can minimize it though. This is an important point for a fair and constructive review process. Training is critical.

BARE ESSENTIAL

ERROR OF SIMILARITY

People tend to like people who think and act like they do. Reviewers may think more highly of other staff members who are most like them and may therefore inflate the ratings they give those employees. As with other errors, this error will be minimized if you properly train your evaluators regarding the standards for evaluation and the use of objective data. Again, always require specific examples to back up a given rating.

ERROR OF STEREOTYPING

This error occurs when a reviewer has an opinion about a group of people and is not able to differentiate among the individuals within that group. A receptionist, for example, may feel that the technician staff as a whole does not work as hard as she does, and consequently, she will rate all technicians equally despite variations in their individual productivity. Ask for specific examples to combat this tendency.

ONE-EXPERIENCE EFFECT

One action may be remembered so vividly that other actions to the contrary are not remembered at all. For example, a normally diligent kennel assistant sends home a soiled dog, resulting in a client complaint. Reviewers may disclude all her diligent work and rate her based on that single episode. This effect is minimized by requiring specific examples to back up all ratings and by jotting progress notes throughout the year.

ELIMINATING ERRORS IN THE WORLD REVIEW

If you are teaching your employees to perform world reviews, you must be clear with them regarding your job standards. Be sure they know this is not an internal contest. It may ease your mind to know that friendship has little influence on confidential responses and that respondents are honest and relatively consistent as long as they are properly trained.

With the world review, you will have a greater chance of catching and eliminating errors through careful scrutiny of the evaluations. When there is little variety in the ratings, rest assured things are running smoothly. When there is great variety among ratings, it is time to look for a problem.

In an effective world review, consider the ratings useful and accurate if there is more than 70 percent agreement among raters. If a rater is attempting to manipulate the system or does not have all the information she needs to complete the evaluation, there may be a scoring discrepancy. If the difference is greater than 30 percent, or more than three points on a ten-point scale, between one evaluator and the others, that evaluator is considered a "discrepant responder." Some error is likely coming into play that you should investigate. Sometimes, two employees will conspire to give each other high ratings. This collusion can be observed easily as you review the evaluation forms.

Because there is a low probability of a highly discrepant responder being right while all other raters are wrong, highly discrepant responders should be discounted. One way to eliminate discrepant responders and thus achieve a valid rating and minimize bias is to use trimmed mean scoring, where the extreme high and low responses are removed from the evaluation. It is possible that a rater has access to information that no other rater has. In this case, the discrepant value may be valid. You may be able to determine the validity of a rating by the detailed comments that accompany that rating. A scoring discrepancy in one or two values is not significant. A discrepancy in many or all values is significant and indicates that the discrepant evaluator should be discounted entirely.

You may want to consider giving feedback to the evaluators themselves. If you can do this while maintaining their anonymity, it might improve the accuracy of the evaluation process over time. It lets evaluators know when their rating has been out of line and gives you an opportunity to retrain them. It is my opinion that guaranteeing anonymity to encourage honest answers is more important than speaking to discrepant responders. If, however, you want to hold discrepant responders accountable for their ratings and retrain them, be sure that you add a place for the rater's name on the review form. Names of evaluators should still be withheld from the employee receiving the appraisal.

SUMMARY

It is best for you and your employees to be aware of the biases and errors that come into play when an employee's performance is being evaluated. Errors can be minimized by conducting world reviews rather than traditional reviews, by using objective data, and by substantiating ratings with specific examples of performance. Errors can also be minimized by properly training evaluators on the standards by which each employee's performance should be judged.

Because you have a data set with the world review, you can evaluate the different responses for the same employee and often see where errors or biases are coming into play. When an evaluator's responses are clearly biased or different from the norm, they should not be included in the evaluation.

CHAPTER 6

COMPLETING THE TRADITIONAL REVIEW FORM

Read this chapter only if you are conducting a traditional review. If you are using a world-review system, you may want to fast-forward to Chapter Seven to avoid repetition.

The traditional review form is most appropriate for practices with five or fewer employees or practices in which the staff and environment do not support a world review. The traditional review is conducted by a single rater who evaluates employees according to whether they have met the requirements of their positions as outlined in their job descriptions. A traditional review form is found on pages 160-161. If you prefer a more detailed form, the world review form can also be used by a single evaluator.

You will be rating each employee in different categories based on whether she meets her job requirements, does not meet requirements, or exceeds requirements for that area. It is important to keep in mind that a good employee will "meet job requirements." This is, after all, what you ask of her. It is a perfectly acceptable rating. "Exceeds job requirements" should be saved for employees who are truly superstars in an area—for employees who can be *objectively* said to do more than the job requires. The employee

47

who "does not meet requirements" will need counseling or training. This employee needs to improve in one or more areas to be a satisfactory employee.

As you go step by step through the evaluation form, use the next few pages, which highlight the performance criteria for different positions and the standards you want to consider for employee evaluation in each area. I have prepared a list of criteria that should fully evaluate all aspects of performance. The standards for some criteria are the same for all positions. Certainly, the technical requirements for a kennel assistant are very different than those for a doctor, yet both should maintain a positive attitude and be punctual.

Use these guidelines as a starting point for your evaluation. Does the employee you are evaluating meet these guidelines? More importantly, does the employee meet your practice's standards in each area as determined in her job description?

Be sure to give your employees a copy of the *Employee's Guide to the Performance Appraisal* that accompanies this book so they can better understand the process as it relates directly to them.

PERFORMANCE CRITERIA

ATTENDANCE/PUNCTUALITY

An employee who meets the standard for her job will always be on time and ready for work at the start of her shift. She is back on time from breaks and does not leave early. A substandard performer would be someone who comes in late, is often sick, or has a habit of asking to leave early. Keep in mind that this is an objective evaluation. You understand that an ill person will not be working. This does not change the fact that an ill employee who is at home is not working to meet hospital goals. An employee who excels in this area is always early for her shift and has not needed time off from her appointed schedule for personal needs. This is one area where you could argue that the best rating should be "meets job requirements," because it is the obligation of all employees to be on time for every shift and to work every scheduled shift. The standard is no different for any position in your hospital.

Client Interaction

The standard here may be different for a kennel assistant than for a receptionist. For a kennel assistant, an appropriate level of client interaction might be to be polite to clients and assist them to their cars when necessary. The standard for a receptionist involves considerably more. For a receptionist to exceed her job requirement in this area, she must really go the extra mile for clients.

All Positions

Common expectations for all positions include:

- greets clients quickly and appropriately
- smiles at clients
- is able to answer general questions clearly and completely
- uses proper English (or the preferred language of the client)
- speaks politely and confidently
- deals effectively with unhappy or disgruntled clients
- speaks clearly
- is able to calm an agitated client
- assists clients when needed
- does not keep clients waiting
- promotes client confidence in the practice

Receptionists

In addition, receptionists should be able to:

- check clients in and out quickly
- have an effective phone manner

- answer the phone by the second ring
- handle multiple phone lines

Technicians

Technicians should also be able to:

- make clients comfortable
- answer any basic questions clients have regarding procedures, medications, and common ailments
- communicate clearly and at the client's level, including putting medical jargon into lay terms

Veterinarians

Veterinarians should also be able to:

- make clients comfortable
- fully answer client questions
- communicate clearly and effectively, including putting medical jargon into lay terms

Managers

A manager should also be able to:

- effectively resolve any client complaint or concern

COMMUNICATION SKILLS

All Positions

The criteria are the same for all positions in your hospital:

- communicate clearly and effectively
- have no problems resulting from miscommunication or misunderstanding
- be familiar with technical and medical words

- have a familiar, comfortable style of communication
- have clear and accurate writing
- use proper notations on cage cards and records

TECHNICAL SKILLS

Clearly, the standard here will be different for each group of employees. Technicians, doctors, and receptionists must be evaluated on whether they have the technical skills needed to fulfill the requirements of their job. These guidelines can be used as a basis for evaluation. I have not included criteria for a veterinary assistant, because the requirements of that position vary tremendously among veterinary practices.

Receptionists

Receptionists must:

- have good typing and processing speed on the computer, be familiar with the practice's computer system, and navigate the practice's computer system capably
- be able to perform irregular tasks, such as printing duplicate rabies certificates and sending reminders
- be able to run end-of-day, end-of-month, and end-of-year reports
- be able to fix minor computer glitches
- be adept at inputting information without error
- be able to accurately process cash, check, and charge transactions

Kennel Assistants

Kennel assistants must be able to:

- perform required cleaning procedures
- handle animals safely, including the correct use of restraint procedures and the proper use of collars and leashes
- administer medication to kenneled pets

Technicians

Veterinary technicians must:

- be proficient at running all in-house lab tests
- be able to perform dental procedures without assistance or supervision (when permitted by state law and hospital policy)
- be fully capable as anesthetic nurses
- be able to take apart your anesthetic machine and put it back together
- be knowledgeable about the intricacies of your monitoring equipment
- be able to take diagnostic-quality radiographs on her first attempt, and be able to adjust radiographic settings to obtain the best picture
- be able to position properly for all radiographic views
- be able to dispense prescription medication
- be capable phlebotomists
- be able to administer injections properly
- be proficient at animal restraint

Veterinarians

The technical skills for your veterinarians will depend on the level of ability you require as well as on available equipment. You cannot evaluate thoracic surgery competency, for example, if your practice refers thoracic cases to a referral practice. Requirements for veterinarians include:

- surgical competency: routine soft tissue, orthopedic, abdominal, thoracic
- ability to perform dental work, including extractions, dental radiographs, and advanced dental procedures
- ability to do venipuncture and centesis
- ability to administer medications and injections
- proficient animal-handling skills

- ability to conduct thorough physical exams, including ophthalmic, otic, and neurologic exams
- ability to provide and alter fluid therapy appropriate to the patient's condition
- diagnostic abilities, including the ability to interpret laboratory values, evaluate blood gas measurements, read radiographs, and read ECGs
- ability to use monitoring equipment properly

Managers

Managers must be able to:

- perform inventory control and management
- evaluate financial and productivity reports
- maintain the computer system
- manage the facility
- create and maintain business data and reports
- plan the future of the practice
- evaluate staffing needs
- evaluate and monitor staff performance
- evaluate current and changing market conditions
- evaluate price structure

KNOWLEDGE BASE

Although each employee requires only a subset of information to function adequately, your hospital will improve as employees expand their knowledge base.

Receptionists

A receptionist should have knowledge of:

- dispensing procedures
- food and supplies sold by the hospital
- cat and dog breeds

- basic health issues
- postoperative instructions
- vaccination and basic health-care protocols

If your receptionist knows how to perform all these tasks, she will appear more confident, professional, knowledgeable, and trustworthy to your clients. She will ask fewer questions of the doctors and technicians. If, however, the job description for your receptionists limits their knowledge base to appointment scheduling and computer invoicing, you must mark that they "meet job expectations" if they have that level of knowledge. Someone who knows all that other information as well will certainly rate as "exceeds requirements," not to mention the fact that she will be a more valuable employee.

Kennel Assistants

Kennel assistants should have knowledge of:

- cleaning compounds
- cage and kennel cleaning procedures
- proper feeding routines
- significant signs of disease or distress in animals

If the assistant has the knowledge to run lab tests and recognize side effects of medications being taken by the kennel animals, she is more valuable to your hospital and exceeds the requirements of the job.

Technicians

Veterinary technicians must have an extensive knowledge base. They should have knowledge of:

- basic anatomy and physiology
- cat and dog breeds

- products used or sold in the practice
- your equipment
- safety issues

Veterinarians

Veterinarians, of course, must have all the knowledge of the veterinary technicians. In addition, they must have detailed knowledge of:

- drugs and products
- medical and surgical techniques

If you are evaluating a veterinarian's knowledge base—a difficult attribute to quantify, to be sure—you might ask yourself whether there have been situations in which it was clear the veterinarian did not have the knowledge to answer a client's question or treat a patient properly.

Managers

Managers must also be knowledgeable regarding:

- marketing practices
- state and federal laws and regulations affecting human resource management and the business environment
- the practice's computer system
- the practice's bookkeeping system
- employee benefits

PRODUCTIVITY

You may have a sense of each employee's productivity, but if you can use objective information, such as the number of procedures performed or the number of appointments booked, you and your employee will be better served. For the productivity evaluation, consider strictly how much work is done by an employee; in other words, how many tasks does the employee complete correctly during a workday? It is important to note that quality of the work must coexist with quantity. If the work performed is of poor quality, more work will be needed to complete or repair the work already performed—a decidedly nonproductive situation. In rare cases (in veterinary practice), employees are capable of completing more work than they are given. That does not factor in here. Rate employees only for the work they actually accomplish.

Receptionists

Receptionists should be rated on:

- the number of appointments booked per day
- the number of clients checked in per day
- the number of clients invoiced per day

Kennel Assistants

Kennel assistants should be rated on:

- the number of animals cared for in a given time

Technicians

Veterinary technicians should be rated on:

- the number of patients seen (where appropriate)
- the number of dentals performed (where appropriate)
- the number of radiographs completed in a given time

Veterinarians

Veterinarians should be rated on:

- the number of patients seen per day
- the number of surgeries and procedures completed per day

Managers

Managers should be rated on:

- the number of transactions completed per day

ATTITUDE

This is an area that needs little introduction. You already know which employees have a good attitude and which do not. The only thing to keep in mind here is that you are rating employees against the requirements of their job. There won't be a great distinction between someone who meets their job requirements and someone who exceeds them, but if an employee's occasional down day or laid-back demeanor does not detract from her work, the employee should receive a satisfactory rating. Your candidate for a top rating will be the cheerful employee who always acts in a way that shows she holds her job, your practice, and your clients in the highest regard.

All Positions

The employee with a good attitude:

- wants to be at work every day
- has a helpful, cheerful demeanor
- has a positive impact on clients so that clients see the employee likes where she works
- has a positive impact on coworkers so they know she is glad to be a part of their team

EFFICIENCY AND ACCURACY

An employee's efficiency, like productivity, is influenced by her speed, knowledge base, dexterity, and motivation. The difference in evaluating efficiency is the economy and adeptness with which an employee performs her duties. Accuracy is another skill that promotes efficiency by saving time and promoting effective communication. Accuracy should be especially evaluated in relation to record keeping, cash-register-drawer management, and labeling and dispensing of medications.

All Positions

The consequence of greater efficiency is greater potential for productivity. Although you may have a sense of each employee's proficiency, there are some objective measures to help. An efficient employee:

- wastes no time or materials
- gets the task done in three steps instead of four

Receptionists

Receptionists can be evaluated on:

- the time it takes to check a client in or out
- the time it takes to run reports
- accuracy of cash handling and financial transactions

Kennel Assistants

Kennel assistants can be evaluated on:

- wasted food or materials
- cleaning time per cage or kennel

Technicians

Evaluate a technician's efficiency based on:

- the time it takes her to run lab tests or to take radiographs
- repeated radiographs and wasted materials

Veterinarians

The efficiency of veterinarians can be partly determined based on:

- the time it takes to complete a surgical procedure
- whether the doctor sees patients in her allotted appointment times

Managers

Hospital managers should be evaluated based on their:

- ability to manage cash
- ability to pay bills in a timely manner
- ability to maintain tight inventory control
- ability to plan accurately for future needs and growth
- ability to handle accounts receivable in an efficient and timely manner
- ability to allocate personnel effectively

PROFESSIONAL APPEARANCE

We live in a society where there is a great range of what people consider appropriate work attire. Younger workers, especially, may not understand your dress code. As a result, many practices must enforce a dress code. For some practices, that means a designated uniform. For others, it means limitations on personal dress. Whatever your standard for your practice, there are general attributes that can be judged.

All Positions

- the employee should arrive in clean, nonstained, nonwrinkled uniforms or clothes

- the employee's hair should not be unkempt
- if an employee has a beard or mustache, it should be trimmed neatly
- the employee must maintain good personal hygiene
- the employee should wear appropriately sized clothes; clothes that are too small are unprofessional; very large or baggy clothes are not only unprofessional, they also present a physical hazard
- skirts and dresses should be an appropriate length
- if your practice requires uniforms, the employees must wear them consistently and keep them in good, professional-appearing condition

While you shouldn't evaluate someone's personal style per se, you do have the right to judge whether her appearance meets your practice's standard for professionalism.

If you choose to limit body piercings (to pierced ears, for example), make your policy clear and consider adding a grandfather clause. An employee might be entitled to keep her body piercings if your policy goes into effect after her employment has already commenced.

It would be difficult to say if any employee deserves an "exceeds expectations" rating in this category. Certainly, some people are more presentable and better dressed than others. Differentiating between an employee who meets your dress-code expectations and one who exceeds them, however, is entirely subjective.

Cleanliness

Some employees frequently clean their areas when they have a moment, while others hardly notice the layer of dust on the shelves even when you point it out to them. Your best employees will do the following:

- keep your lab equipment meticulously clean to ensure its proper functioning
- clean the dust on the bottle of medicine they are about to dispense before they hand it over to the client
- mop up "accidents" in the waiting room before you even know there was one

Employees need to recognize that cleanliness contributes to a sanitary practice environment, provides a pleasant atmosphere for workers and clients, and maintains the equipment and facility. Make sure they are all doing their share and rate them accordingly.

ORGANIZATION

It may be more difficult for you to evaluate your employee's organizational skills. Sometimes it is easier to notice the end result of disorganization: the employee who can't remember where she put something, the incomplete surgery logs, and the poorly kept client communication notes. It is also difficult to establish the standard of organization for each job. This must be a subjective evaluation. I suggest that an acceptable level of organization is one that allows for efficient performance and that prevents errors or absences in record keeping or patient care.

Employee Responsible for the Pharmacy:

- ensures that medications are well organized and easily found
- makes it clear where backup products are located

Receptionists:

- organize the appointment schedule to promote on-time service and optimal client care

Technicians:

- organize each day's surgery schedule to maximize use of your time
- coordinate treatments, diagnostics, and laboratory procedures

Veterinarians:

- organize call-backs and unplanned procedures to best mesh with scheduled appointments and procedures
- perform all procedures in an organized manner

Managers:

- organize staff schedules to maximize efficient practice operations
- organize the office so that items are easy to locate

Beware of the extreme organizer. There comes a point when what seems like organization does not deserve a higher rating because it is so *inefficient*. If you have an employee who tracks *everything* and seems to have a dozen lists going, you either have a bad computer system or an extreme organizer.

COOPERATION

You couldn't get through the day without cooperation from your staff—at least, you wouldn't want to. As cooperation among your team members improves, you increase the efficiency of your practice and make it a more pleasant environment for your staff and your clients. I love a staff member who sees her role broadly as serving clients and helping doctors rather than narrowly as a kennel assistant or receptionist.

The only time cooperation is not beneficial is when an employee sacrifices her own duties to help perform someone else's. For example, your budding technician, currently employed as a kennel assistant, may take too many opportunities to assist your technicians.

For purposes of the review, the employee who meets the expectations of her job will:

- work with other employees to gather information and to complete tasks
- jump in and take over when another employee is called to a second task

Someone who does *not* meet expectations:

- does not share information that would help other employees
- does not offer to help others complete their tasks
- may not help others even when directly asked for help

The employee who *exceeds* expectations can always be counted on to lend a hand and seamlessly jump in when she sees a need she can fill.

INITIATIVE

All your employees should show initiative, although the appropriate amount varies among hospitals. You certainly do not want your employees to have *so* much initiative that they buy new computer software for the practice or start giving away services without your approval. You do, however, want all your employees to have enough initiative to suggest better ways of working and to be able to handle an emergency situation on their own. You want your kennel assistant to have enough initiative to find productive work to do when there are not many patients and boarders.

I was away at a meeting one afternoon. I came back to the hospital about 5 P.M. to check on a patient and finish some paperwork. As I walked in the front door, I saw my two receptionists using towels to mop up water on the floor behind the desk. Boxes from the supply closet had been moved out and items hung to dry. A water pipe had burst. Before I even knew about it, the receptionists had figured out how to turn off the water, had called the plumber the practice normally uses, and had performed damage control on the items near the burst pipe. That's the kind of initiative I want my employees to have—not to overstep their bounds, but to go ahead and get things done without having to be told to do them.

All Positions

An employee who "meets requirements":

- finds productive work without being specifically directed
- solves any crisis to which she would reasonably be exposed in her position

Receptionists

Receptionists who "meet job requirements" in the area of initiative:

- keep busy when things are slow
- offer to assist clients

Technicians

Technicians who have enough initiative:

- maintain patient care in the absence of a veterinarian; for example, to withhold a scheduled oral medication if a pet vomits until she can check with the veterinarian or to deliver oxygen by mask to a cat in asthmatic crisis that has just been rushed in the door while the doctor is notified

Veterinarians

Veterinarians must absolutely have the initiative to:

- make decisions regarding patient care/treatment
- address client or staff issues

COMPLETING THE TRADITIONAL REVIEW FORM

Managers

Managers must have enough initiative to:

- resolve client complaints
- deal with facility emergencies
- alter the business plan to address changing market conditions and available personnel
- initiate marketing efforts to bond clients, increase client base, and promote optimal service

ADAPTABILITY

What is an acceptable level of adaptability? It all depends on your practice. If nothing ever changes at your practice, your employees may not need to be very flexible in order to meet your expectations. If, however, things are constantly changing at your practice, your employees need the flexibility of a world class gymnast. In all likelihood, your practice lies somewhere in-between. Your employees need to be able to adapt to the various requests and demands of your clients as well as to changes in practice policy and services.

Some employees just won't change. Even when you explain the reason for the change and train them in the new protocol, they still will not adapt to a new system. You may spend more time on these employees than necessary, and you don't have the consistency you need in your practice. These employees get your lowest score for adaptability. Employees who immediately adapt to any changes instigated and who reinforce the changes with your other employees get your best rating.

OVERALL PERFORMANCE

Once you have rated each employee on all aspects of her job, you need to put the ratings all together. This is discussed in more detail in Chapter Nine. Be aware, however, that you should not rate every aspect equally. A receptionist's ability to interact effectively with clients is more important than the degree of initiative she shows. A surgical technician's knowledge base and technical abilities should weigh more heavily than her appearance.

REVIEW PRIOR GOALS

It is now time to gather the last bits of information you need to put the evaluation together and provide an overall assessment of the employee's progress. Pull out her last review. If the employee has been with you less than a year, take out her review from the end of her trial period. Look at the goals you set at that review.

Write down all of the goals the employee met and all those she did not. If the goals and time frame to meet them were reasonable, there should be only one list. If the employee did not meet goals, consider carefully why that occurred.

- Did she not take the goals seriously?
- Were they only your goals and never important to her?
- Did something happen to alter the time frame in which it would be reasonable for her to accomplish her goals?
- Did anything change at your practice that altered the goals you wanted this employee to achieve? For example, if one of your goals was to have the employee learn a certain procedure on your computer, but you changed computer systems, the goal may be moot. If the employee was out on sick leave for three months and was not able to attend a planned continuing-education meeting, you should not penalize her for the unmet goal.

DETERMINE THE EMPLOYEE'S STRENGTHS

Next, evaluate what you believe to be this employee's strengths. The easiest way to do this is to look where you rated her highly on the evaluation form. Be specific. If one of your receptionist's strengths is her skill with client interactions, determine the exact circumstances that bring out that strength. Perhaps it is that she manages to pleasantly accommodate even the most trying client. Perhaps it is that she always smiles when she is talking to callers, which really comes across as a friendly attitude.

Why is it so important to be precise and give exact examples? If you can say to your receptionist that she did a really great job last week when Mrs. Jones was horribly upset about her bill, then the receptionist's behavior will be reinforced. You will also know the exact situations in which you can utilize her strengths and which of her behaviors can set an example for other members of your staff.

Where should you look for the strengths of other employees? Again, go back to the first part of your review form. Did you rate your technician highly for her knowledge base? Why, specifically, is that? Did she know how to maximize the chance of a positive *giardia* fecal float when you didn't? Were you impressed with her knowledge of different anesthetics? As you rate your kennel assistant, ask yourself if she got top ratings for animal handling. Specifically, how did the assistant show her expertise?

There are two points here. The first is that you want your employees to know exactly where you feel they are succeeding in their job. The second is that you want to interpret how each employee's strengths can maximize your hospital's performance. Will one employee's strong suit be used to train other employees? Can you ensure that the strongest employee will be handling every client and every task?

FOR BEST RESULTS

Once you have thought so specifically about the employee's strong points and goals, take a step back and look at the big picture. What was a major achievement for this employee this year? Did your practice manager successfully cut inventory costs? Did your technician gain a new skill? Did a receptionist take charge of the client newsletter? Mark down any significant achievement. It will help you recognize what has been accomplished this year and pass that recognition on to the employee as well as provide a record of the year's events.

DETERMINE WHERE THE EMPLOYEE NEEDS IMPROVEMENT

That takes care of all the good things you want to discuss with the employee. A more complicated area is deciding where this employee can focus her attention for the coming year. This area used to be called "weaknesses," but now it is usually referred to as "areas that need improvement" or "opportunities for further development." All of us have areas in which we can improve. Some of them are related to our jobs, and some are not. There may even be "weak" areas in your employee's personality you wish you could change. You can't. All you can change are behaviors that directly impact her job performance.

Here again, you must be specific. It will not help your receptionist if you say she is having trouble with the rest of the staff. In fact, it will probably hurt her relationships with them further. You will be productive in your evaluation if you can identify specific problem areas in which she can improve. For example, if she is having trouble with other staff members because she is always the first one to leave at the end of the shift, you can set some guidelines for her. If the problem is that she never pitches in and helps others but always expects their cooperation and assistance, you have given her a specific problem to consider and work on improving. These opportunities for improvement are going to roll over into your goals for this employee for the coming year.

Perhaps your receptionist has never worked in a veterinary practice before. While she is doing well with the clients, she does not have enough knowledge of products and medications. As often happens in veterinary practices, this receptionist hit the ground running and was not given thorough training. She is learning as she goes. She still is not always able to answer basic questions posed by clients, such as, "Which shampoo would be best for my schnauzer?" "Can you recommend something for dry skin?" "What would work for my cat's hairballs?" This receptionist has been rated as "not meeting job requirements" in the knowledge category. Under development needs, you have noted that she needs to increase working knowledge of your products. For her goals, you might say that she is to begin studying product labels and inserts. You might assign someone of whom she may ask questions while she is learning. Write down that you are giving her three or six months (or whatever seems reasonable in your practice) to accomplish this goal.

Maybe you are reviewing your kennel assistant, who is a working mom, and have given her unsatisfactory marks for punctuality. While she is there, she does a great job, but her tardiness is a problem. A reasonable future goal is for her to be on time for every shift, starting tomorrow. In this circumstance, you do not need to make a plan to accomplish the goal—your employee does.

Other times, you will need a plan of action to help your employee meet the goals you are setting. For instance, perhaps you have been attending lectures on physical therapy (PT) for dogs and really want to bring this into your practice. You need your technician to learn about PT so that she can perform many of the treatments. Her future goal will be to learn PT and carry out this added service. How are you going to help her accomplish this goal? Are you going to set aside your own time to teach her? Are you going to send her to a continuing-education program where PT will be emphasized?

Based on how you rated your employees, there may be areas in which they could improve that are difficult to translate into developmental opportunities or goals. If a staff member does not have the initiative to find productive work during slow periods, your goal is obvious—have the employee show more initiative. However, it is not as easy to teach someone initiative as it is to teach her how to clean a cage or take a radiograph. In these situations, you will have to depend on your employee to take steps on her own. You could start by giving her a list of things that could be accomplished during slow times. Ultimately, initiative is a trait that your employee must develop for herself.

Achievements, weak areas, and goals all get marked on the review form. Chapter Eight has a more complete discussion of goals and goal setting—the end focus of the review discussion.

Summary

Having chosen the traditional review, the onus falls squarely on you, the supervisor, to fairly and thoroughly evaluate your employee's performance. Gather performance data and specific examples of the employee's work. Rate your employee against all criteria, using her job description as your standard for whether she meets the requirements of her job. After completing the actual ratings, complete the review by noting highlights from the review period and areas that demand attention. The goals you set for this employee should be based on areas that require improvement, as well as on the needs of your practice for the future.

CHAPTER 7

COMPLETING THE WORLD REVIEW FORM

If you are conducting a traditional review, you do not need to read this chapter and may wish to go directly to Chapter Eight.

For those of you conducting world reviews for the first time, you have taken on a bit of a challenge. Once the process is in place and accepted, the review should move fairly seamlessly. In the initial stages, however, there is often hesitation because it is uncomfortable to do something new. It will take your staff some time—probably two review cycles—to feel comfortable with the world review and have all their questions or concerns addressed. The information you gain with a world review is extremely valuable, as long as the evaluators have been instructed properly.

This chapter presents information on the design of a world review form and the standard against which employees are evaluated. It also provides step-by-step details on filling out the evaluation form itself. The evaluation form followed in this chapter is found on pages 151-153. You can use these comments and guidelines to build a training seminar for your staff. Also, give your employees the *Employee's Guide to the Performance Appraisal* that accompanies this book so they can better understand the process as it relates directly to them.

Because the world review consolidates the feedback of many evaluators who work with an employee, it should be more specific in its evaluation than a traditional review. You do not want to have to divine the thoughts or intent of the evaluators. Your employees do not have much experience or training in evaluating other employees. Therefore, they need to have as clear and simple a process as possible. It is important that you emphasize in your staff training the need for raters to be *specific* when they make comments in their evaluations.

The rating scale is different for a world review than it is for a traditional format. You are rating an employee not just against her job standard, but against the ideal employee—the perfect ten. All she needs to do to be a good employee is to perform to the standards of her job. Be very clear on that, because it is an important legal point. For job retention, an employee must meet the requirements of her position. Still, you want her to know how much room there is for improvement to achieve superstar-employee status.

VARIATIONS ON STANDARDS FOR THE WORLD REVIEW

Earlier in the book, it was mentioned that there are many different types of reviews. Although this book covers the two most commonly accepted frameworks for a review, you may certainly create variations of them. In your practice, you may wish to alter the evaluation standard used for the world review. The traditional review uses the standard of what an employee needs to do to meet her job requirements as described in her job description. You can certainly use that standard for the world review as well. You can also evaluate each employee against the highest standard for her particular position. For example, a technician would be evaluated against a theoretical superstar technician, or a manager against the most impressive manager. Never use comparisons among your own staff members for your evaluations.

I strongly recommend a different standard for the world review. You have chosen the world review because teamwork and employee empowerment are important to you. You want to reap the benefits of a system that supports a commitment to continuous learning and that maximizes organizational effectiveness. Veterinary practices are unique in that most call upon employees to perform tasks outside the domain of the employee's stated job. Veterinary practices cross-train heavily. They are not like the human hospitals, where a receptionist is always a receptionist and a radiographic technician does nothing but take radiographs. Veterinary-practice receptionists are sometimes salespeople, sometimes laboratory staff, sometimes animal restrainers, and sometimes janitors. Technicians are often called upon as nurses, laboratory assistants, exam-room assistants, client counselors, radiographic technicians, and inventory managers.

In that spirit, the best employees—the best team members—are going to be those who can fill multiple roles at the practice. Employees are more valuable when they have a broader range of skills. The best team member can answer the phone as well as the best receptionist and can take a diagnostic-quality radiograph on the first try. It is true that a receptionist needs the best client-communication skills. Although a technician may use those skills less frequently, it is still critical that her client interactions be positive and successful. A receptionist with animal-handling skills is more valuable than one who can't hold a cat still for a blood draw when you are the only two employees in the practice. A veterinarian is not hired on the basis of organizational skills, but the organized veterinarian will be more efficient and productive and will create fewer headaches for other staff members. There are skills that don't seem critical, on the surface, to performing a specific job. But they are indeed important to having the successful practice you desire.

Your standard for the world review, then, should be the fictional ideal employee—fictional, because an employee honestly cannot reach a perfect score in every category. There are areas in which there are trade-offs—you give up a small amount of success in one to increase success in another. However, the perfect-ten employee is the one you need to have in mind when you conduct your review. This is the receptionist who is always perfectly groomed, who is adored by clients without a single complaint, and who is efficient and liked by all the staff. She can run laboratory tests and monitor surgical patients as effectively as she can run computer reports. That's the kind of employee you should have in mind as you complete your evaluation. All employees are rated by this same standard. As a result, every employee should be evaluated using the same form without modification.

NUMERICAL RATING SCALE

Regarding the numerical rating scale, I prefer to rate employees from 1 to 10. It is a range with which people are comfortable working. People are also used to thinking in terms of the "perfect 10." If you have a wider range, it becomes less meaningful. If you have a narrower range, say 1 to 5, people tend to want to rate people in between numbers in some categories. "She's not quite a perfect 5, but she's better than a 4. I'll give her a 4½." As with most scales, 1 indicates the lowest possible performance—a very poor rating. A 10 is perfection. There is no longer any room for improvement if someone rates a 10. Consequently, employees should very rarely, if ever, receive a 10. That would be equivalent to saying that the employee is so strong or effective in that area she could never do any better. Do you think that is ever true? No more room for increased cooperation? Could not improve her attitude? Could not possibly know anything else?

People may be able to reach the performance of an ideal employee in one specific area, but often to the detriment of another area. Consequently, your best employees will rate highly in all areas but are unlikely to receive 10s. For example, the employee who is the most pleasant with clients and makes them feel cared for is likely to spend more time interacting with clients. The speed of her transactions will then suffer. There is often a balance among ideals.

A midlevel rating of 5 should be given to employees who perform adequately in the area you are rating. Their performance is acceptable, but they still have room for improvement. For any rating below 5, you should be thinking ahead to setting a goal for improvement in that area as well as developing a plan for your employee to achieve that goal. Keep in mind that your ideal employee is going to be highly rated in all areas regardless of how certain skills are utilized. She may only do a certain procedure once a year, but she deserves credit for her ability to do it.

The world review presented here is broken down into different performance areas that are further broken down into specific traits that impact a certain performance area. By getting more specific, it is difficult for an employee's subjective opinions to come into play. For example, if you ask Sarah about Mary's knowledge base, Sarah may at first think that it is quite extensive and may give her a 9. After all, Mary is the person to whom she goes when she has a question. However, when you break it down further, Sarah realizes that Mary should get a 9 for her knowledge of the products you sell, but she rates only a 5 for her technical knowledge, because she cannot perform any lab or surgical procedures.

Similarly, your employees may feel that Sarah is a strong team member. She gets along well with everybody and tries to help fellow employees whenever she can. When your employees rate Sarah on the team skill of "does not avoid any aspect of job," however, they remember that they always let her get away with not mopping the waiting area because she dislikes it so much. It allows them to realize that they can't give Sarah the high rating they thought they would at first.

EXPLANATION OF SPECIFIC AREAS FOR EVALUATION

The next few pages walk through the specific areas for evaluation and offer suggestions for specific criteria you can use in your determination of a rating. Match the criterion with its line on your evaluation sheet and use the listed standards to determine where on the 1-to-10 scale the employee belongs. All of the traits that contribute to the best veterinary staff are included in the evaluation. Some traits will be more important to you than others. You may even find other characteristics you would like to add to your own evaluation, particularly if you are using the review as part of a strategy to address target areas in your practice. Characteristics included here are relevant to every position at your hospital.

Two positions require additional evaluation: managers and veterinarians. Managers or supervisors must have their leadership and supervisory skills evaluated. They also should be evaluated for their contribution to facility maintenance, financial management, and employee morale. Veterinarians also need an in-depth evaluation of their medical and surgical skills. Only veterinary colleagues, the practice manager, or the owner should perform this additional evaluation. Nonveterinary owners and managers may find it difficult to evaluate a veterinarian's skill well. Staff and client comments or complaints may be useful in highlighting strengths and weaknesses. Industry benchmarks might also be used to aid in evaluation. For example, the American Animal Hospital Association publishes a report (*Financial and Productivity Pulsepoints: A Comprehensive Survey and Analysis of Benchmark and Performance Data*) that breaks down income by profit centers such as laboratory, dentistry, and radiography. If the dentistry revenue (determined as a percent of sales) is much lower than the benchmark, dentistry may be a potential growth area for your veterinarian.

By using numbers in the evaluation, it will be easy to track your employees' progress from year to year. Numerical ratings can also be used as the basis for an incentive program. Unless you find some confusion or major error with your review form, it is preferable to use the same form from year to year. That is the only way you will be able to properly track changes from one review period to the next.

PERFORMANCE CRITERIA

CLIENT RELATIONS

Has Good Phone Manner and Skills

- answers the phone on the first or second ring
- uses the proper greeting
- smiles while talking on the phone
- manages multiple phone lines at once
- comes across as pleasant and knowledgeable
- speaks clearly and properly
- is effective with phone shoppers
- does not keep clients holding
- does not say "uh" or "you know"

Deals with Clients Quickly and Efficiently

- triages incoming clients
- checks clients in and out quickly
- finds files and paperwork quickly
- keeps client conversations "on track"
- does not keep clients waiting in the exam room

Is Pleasant to Clients

- acknowledges clients as soon as they arrive
- uses clients' and pets' names when talking to them

- makes clients feel comfortable
- addresses client questions and concerns
- smiles at clients
- offers to assist clients with a troublesome pet or in carrying products

KNOWLEDGE BASE

Has Knowledge of Products Sold and Dispensed

- has good working knowledge of the products in inventory
- helps clients differentiate between over-the-counter products to determine what is best for their pets
- knows the uses of different medications
- is able to explain to a client the potential side effects of a medication dispensed for the pet

Has Knowledge of Basic Medical Problems and Policies and Procedures

- answers routine client questions without the benefit of a doctor's input
- files accurately
- handles incoming and outgoing mail
- knows hospital procedures, such as opening and closing routines
- has thorough understanding of normal animal behavior, vaccinations, and parasites

Has Knowledge of Technical Procedures

- takes diagnostic-quality radiographs
- is an effective anesthetist
- runs lab tests
- performs dental procedures
- mixes and prepares medications
- gives medications via all routes

Has Computer Knowledge

- invoices clients and creates estimates for services
- runs reports and reminder cards
- pulls the client's file up to an active screen
- inputs reminders effectively
- troubleshoots computer problems
- backs up computer files
- recalls messages from the answering machine and changes the message
- can compile information from the data base to list the best clients or clients who have geriatric pets

Wants to Learn

- actively shows an interest in increasing her skills and knowledge base by asking questions, reading, and attending meetings
- asks questions when she sees someone performing a new procedure or when she sees a new product
- attends all in-house meetings and seminars
- seeks outside continuing education

Is Able to Learn

- comprehends new things quickly and easily
- performs new procedures without having to be shown multiple times

TEAM SKILLS

Has a Good Attitude

- wants to be at work every day; this attitude is observed by clients
- interacts pleasantly and effectively with the rest of the staff
- respects other staff members
- is a cheerleader for the practice

Is Cooperative

- is willing to assist other staff members
- follows through when asked for assistance or when she offers assistance
- covers holiday shifts or absences of other employees when asked

Does Not Avoid Any Aspect of Job

- performs every duty required of her position
- performs duties she finds unpleasant
- performs all tasks, not just one in order to force another employee to perform the alternate task by default

GENERAL SKILLS

Communicates Effectively

- is easily understood
- is not misunderstood
- avoids inappropriate comments and language
- speaks clearly
- has a sufficient vocabulary of medical and animal terms
- expresses medical information in lay terms
- has legible handwriting
- writes clearly and concisely
- is a polished, confident, persuasive speaker
- disagrees without arguing
- does not mumble or say "uh"

Has Effective Animal Handling Skills

- works with the variety of species you see
- keeps pets calm and comfortable

- restrains animals so that neither the person nor the animal is injured
- restrains with finesse rather than with force
- knows the different holds for drawing blood and for procedures such as radiographs and centesis
- demonstrates comfort in handling animals
- one key test for that super handler: would you want this employee to be the only thing between you and a vicious dog or a fractious cat?

Is Efficient, Productive, and Accurate

- gets the job done right the first time so that it will not have to be repeated
- is precise with spoken and written word
- accurately charts patient and client information and keeps accurate records
- accurately processes cash, check, and charge transactions
- completes the maximum possible number of transactions and procedures in one day
- does not waste materials
- keeps the money drawer balanced at the end of every shift
- accurately labels and dispenses medications

Is Punctual and Dependable

- is in position and ready to work every time her shift starts

Maintains Composure

- does not become frazzled during a hectic day
- remains polite and keeps a neutral voice when dealing with a difficult client
- calmly admits a mistake
- handles an emergency calmly and with finesse

Responds Well to Feedback/Comments

- does not interrupt when receiving feedback
- does not immediately try to defend her action or position
- listens carefully first to all you have to say, then asks appropriate questions or responds to your comment
- works with you to correct any problem you have identified
- does not take feedback personally, and does not become disgruntled or withdrawn

Is Adaptable

- performs effectively despite changing policies and procedures
- adapts speech and mannerisms to each client
- easily accepts changes you are trying to make
- is flexible with clients regarding practice policy when appropriate
- adapts to the variety of approaches and techniques used in the practice

Takes Initiative

- finds productive work to do on a slow day
- makes suggestions for improving the practice or for reaching out to clients
- attempts to solve problems as they arise rather than waiting for someone else to solve them

Exercises Good Judgment

- uses common sense and good judgment
- uses discretionary power appropriately when dealing with client requests or complaints
- effectively assesses situations, including identifying troubled clients, faulty equipment, and problems with boarded or hospitalized pets
- uses good judgment in extending credit to clients

Handles Multiple Tasks Concurrently

- effectively handles competing priorities
- handles multiple phone lines
- invoices a client while carrying on a conversation
- monitors multiple patients
- monitors a surgical patient while handling other tasks
- keeps track of verbal instructions while cleaning or performing a procedure or task

Has a Presentable, Professional Appearance

- conforms to hospital dress code
- always wears a clean, unwrinkled uniform
- if uniforms are not required, always wears clean, pressed clothes
- keeps hair neat and makeup and jewelry simple
- keeps beard or mustache neatly trimmed

Maintains a Clean Working Environment

- is diligent about cleaning messes as they occur
- uses proper cleaning supplies to maintain hospital-grade cleanliness and sanitation
- keeps own work area free of dirt, dust, and clutter

Follows Instructions Well

- follows standard hospital protocols and safety guidelines
- complies with instructions to alter protocol
- reads printed instructions and follows them
- when given verbal instruction for tasks, completes the tasks accurately without further instruction

EVALUATING VETERINARIANS AND MANAGERS

The standard review form covers many, if not most, of the skills and traits you should evaluate for managers and veterinarians. However, there is an additional level of evaluation for these positions. The depth of the evaluation depends on the roles people in these positions play at your practice.

MANAGERS

With the tremendous variation in responsibilities for managers, there is not one standard appropriate form that might be used; therefore, none is offered here. At some practices, the manager is also the veterinarian-owner. At others, the manager is given limited responsibilities focusing on personnel and organization. At yet other practices, there may be more than one manager, and these managers may take on a full range of responsibilities, from strategic planning to human resource and financial management.

The duties and skills described in the following pages apply to someone in a management role. I recommend selecting those items that apply to your manager and adding them to your evaluation. For example, if you have an employee with supervisory duties alone, you would select appropriate items from the Human Resources section. If your manager handles a diverse group of duties but does not participate in forecasting or strategic planning, you would simply exclude the inapplicable skills from the evaluation form.

The effects of good management will certainly be observed by the staff and reflected in their evaluations of the manager. Indeed, there are many aspects of business management that the staff would be competent to evaluate. These include successful inventory management, the ability to retain employees, and accounts receivable handling. However, there are many skills that can be evaluated by objective data alone, such as employee retention, accounts receivable handling, and success in increasing the number of clients. For many other skills, only the owner will be in a position to conduct a complete evaluation, such as for bookkeeping and forecasting skills. For these reasons, it is appropriate for the evaluation of management-specific skills to be limited to the owner, to partners, or to superior managers.

Has Planning and Strategy Skills

- develops long-term plans, including material and personnel requirements
- plans appropriate cash flow

Has Marketing Skills

- evaluates and modifies the fee structure
- develops successful advertising and promotional material and/or campaigns
- is an effective public relations agent for the practice
- conducts, evaluates, and utilizes market and consumer analyses

Has Human Resource Skills

- successfully hires desirable applicants
- trains and develops staff
- retains employees
- ensures optimal allocation of personnel
- is familiar with state and federal employment regulations
- is familiar with all available employee benefits
- provides adequate but not overbearing supervision of staff
- evaluates staff regularly
- is a role model and leader for other employees
- leads staff toward set goals
- motivates staff to do their best work
- initiates appropriate staff rewards and incentives

Has Financial Skills

- maintains financial records in a complete, timely, and accurate manner
- minimizes accounts receivable
- allocates funds properly
- manages inventory successfully
- interprets and evaluates financial reports
- provides the accountant with all necessary information
- reassesses expenses in a timely manner and develops methods to minimize expenses

Has General Managerial Skills

- provides for effective facility and computer maintenance
- is familiar with state and federal safety and environmental regulations
- develops schedules for the practice that maximize employee time and effectiveness
- is effective at setting, maintaining, and improving office procedures and filing and record-keeping systems
- upholds the practice mission statement
- provides quality control

VETERINARIANS

Staff members have a good sense for the capabilities of each veterinarian. They see it in happy clients or in poor outcomes. This general sense translates into their evaluations of a veterinarian especially with regard to knowledge base and technical skills.

FOR BEST RESULTS

Staff members, however, are ill equipped to fully evaluate a veterinarian's knowledge or skills. The best evaluator will be another veterinarian who works closely with the veterinarian being evaluated or a veterinarian-owner.

Completing the World Review Form

It is reasonable to expect any veterinarian to be up-to-date on all medical procedures. The depth of knowledge needed in specific areas, however, will depend on the level of care provided at your practice. The skills and knowledge required of an emergency doctor are much different than those required for a doctor working for a low-cost spay-neuter-vaccination practice.

Suggested specific areas of evaluation follow. The list should be tailored to your practice and the level of care you expect. It should also be tailored to include skills for any specialized equipment you might have, such as ultrasound or laser surgery equipment. You might also find it useful to review a few common and a few challenging cases the veterinarian has seen since the last review.

Has Medical Skills

- uses medications prudently
- provides accurate and timely diagnoses
- provides an optimal treatment plan with good results
- has minimal treatment failures
- provides quick, accurate diagnosis and treatment in emergencies
- has full knowledge of all applicable medical and surgical procedures
- works quickly but with great accuracy
- experiences minimal complications
- is able to handle complex procedures

ASKING FOR COMMENTS

Comments are a critical part of the evaluation if you are to help an employee improve her performance. Provide specific examples of the employee's work. For areas in which the employee excels, comments will help reward and reinforce the behavior. For areas in which the employee could develop further, comments will provide specific examples to help. For any area in which the employee was given a

A PRACTICAL GUIDE TO PERFORMANCE APPRAISALS

rating of less than 5 (on the scale of 1 to 10), the rater must provide specific feedback to defend the rating. This will help you advise your reviewee and ensure that the rating is legitimately deserved.

The more specific the comment, the more useful it is. For example, "Needs to be nice to clients" is not particularly helpful. It does not tell the employee specific ways in which she can improve her performance. What would be more helpful is a group of comments like, "Needs to smile at clients," "Needs to call clients by name," and "Needs to maintain composure when talking to demanding clients." Demanding these specific comments for low ratings helps the employee focus on development and provides substantiation for discharge due to poor performance.

Use comments for good performance as well. Highlight what the employee does well. "I consider Mary a role model for friendly interaction with clients." "Sarah did a great job of handling Mrs. Jones' difficult cat." "Jennifer is often out with the mop cleaning up accidents before a client has even brought the accident to our attention." "Anne, I am always so impressed with the way you handle clients who are late for their appointments. You always find some way to keep us on schedule and subtly encourage the client to be more respectful of our schedule."

You may choose to require your employees and supervisors to add specific comments to *any* ratings. That would certainly help maximize feedback for the rated employee and identify what makes an employee successful in her position. Another alternative is to require specific comments for ratings of 4 or below and 9 or above.

TALLYING THE RESULTS

Once you have completed your world evaluation for the employee, and all employees have filled out their forms, it's time to tally the results. Table 7-1 provides examples for summarizing your results. This form is also provided on the disk that accompanies this book.

- For each category, take the numerical average of the answers. For phone manner, one employee receives ratings of 5, 7, 5, 6, and 7. Her average rating for phone manner is a 6. Record this average on a new evaluation form that will be your summary sheet (Table 7-1).
- Transfer any comments to the summary sheet, excluding the irrelevant or repetitive. It is important to maintain the anonymity of the evaluators if you wish your staff to continue giving honest appraisals. Whenever possible, specific examples given to an employee should leave the author indeterminate, even if this requires the examples to be rewritten.
- You might also choose to average scores within each section (Client Relations, Knowledge Base, Team Skills, and General Skills) to help the employee see her performance in a broad sense.

Write down the goals that you and the employee had set at the last review. Check whether or not each goal has been met. You are now ready to summarize the results for your meeting with the employee.

What should you do if your rating is markedly different from the rating of all other evaluators? Consider whether you are the only witness to situations where the attribute is exhibited. For example, a doctor would have better knowledge of an exam-room assistant's ability to restrain animals and interact with clients than the rest of the staff. In this case, if you are the doctor, you should put a star next to that attribute to remind yourself that you must weigh your rating more heavily. Your rating will be used as the basis for discussion under these circumstances. Use of the star should apply to any discrepant responder who has intimate knowledge of an employee's work. If the review is anonymous, however, the reviewer will not be able to make that determination.

Remember, though, that if a given attribute will be displayed to all the staff in a variety of situations, your evaluation may be

Note: This form is also available on the disk that accompanies this book. Please feel free to modify it for your needs.

TABLE 7-1
SUMMARIZING THE RESULTS

This table allows for five reviewers. Boxes may be added or removed to match your number of reviewers.

Client Relations	1	2	3	4	5	Average
Has good phone manner and skills	6	7	6	5	6	6.0
Deals with clients quickly and efficiently	7	6	8	6	6	6.6
Is pleasant to clients	6	7	7	6	6	6.4
Summary Average for Client Relation Skills						**6.3**
Knowledge Base						
Has knowledge of products sold and dispensed	8	7	8	8	8	7.8
Has knowledge of basic medical problems and policies and procedures	7	6	6	7	7	6.6
Has knowledge of technical procedures	4	5	5	6	4	4.8
Has computer knowledge	8	8	9	7	8	8.0
Wants to learn	6	7	8	5	7	6.6
Is able to learn	8	8	7	7	7	7.4
Summary Average for Knowledge Base						**6.9**
Team Skills						
Has a good attitude	5	6	5	4	7	5.4
Is cooperative	5	5	5	5	5	5.0
Does not avoid any aspect of job	8	7	8	6	7	7.2
Summary Average for Team Skills						**5.9**

TABLE 7-1 (cont'd)
SUMMARIZING THE RESULTS

This table allows for five reviewers. Boxes may be added or removed to match your number of reviewers.

General Skills	1	2	3	4	5	Average
Communicates effectively	6	7	5	6	6	6.0
Has effective animal handling skills	2	3	3	4	4	3.2
Is efficient, productive, and accurate	7	8	7	6	7	7.0
Is punctual and dependable	7	7	8	7	7	7.2
Maintains composure	5	4	5	4	4	4.4
Responds well to feedback/ comments	4	5	4	4	4	4.2
Is adaptable	5	5	6	5	5	5.2
Takes initiative	7	7	8	8	8	7.6
Exercises good judgment	6	7	7	5	6	6.2
Handles multiple tasks concurrently	8	8	8	7	8	7.8
Has a presentable, professional appearance	9	9	8	8	7	8.2
Maintains a clean working environment	7	8	7	7	8	7.4
Follows instructions well	6	6	7	7	6	6.4
Summary Average for General Skills						**6.2**

Summary Average for All Attributes   6.3

Comments:

incorrect. The additional information from other evaluators should help you reassess your position. In other words, do not *assume* you are most correct.

The manager-supervisor-evaluator must ultimately provide an evaluation they believe is most accurate after gathering objective data and subjective evaluations. Remember—several parts of the review are inherently subjective; that is why the world review has the advantage in providing several subjective viewpoints and, hopefully, productive comments.

SUMMARIZING THE RESULTS

ATTENDANCE

State simply whether or not your employee's record of attendance is satisfactory. If it is not, this should definitely be a point of discussion during the employee review. A satisfactory attendance record means that the employee is in position ready to work at the beginning of each scheduled shift, that she doesn't leave early, and that she doesn't return late from a break. Make allowances for tardiness *only* for unexpected situations, such as a car accident or slippery roads.

OVERALL NUMERICAL RATING

Summarize the employee's numerical rating for all categories. Add the score for each of the categories together and divide by the number of categories to arrive at the average rating. Although each employee will have weak and strong areas that you will discuss, this will give both you and the employee an idea of her overall standing. Overall, is she a "5" employee or a "9" employee? Most important, how have her ratings moved from one year to the next? Do her numbers get higher over time? They should.

STRENGTHS

Use all the comments and ratings you have compiled to list the employee's strengths. This is where all the comments made by other staff members will be particularly helpful. You can tell by a 7 or better numerical rating that the employee is particularly effective in that area. The comments will tell you specifically how that is so. You hope all of your receptionists receive high ratings for client relations. One, however, may truly excel in phone skills. Therefore, one of her strengths would be listed as "phone communication with clients." Add a note under the strength that the employee is always seen smiling while she is on the phone and how she always uses the caller's name during the conversation. Add that she seems to have great success booking phone shoppers. Perhaps your kennel assistant receives a high rating under "desire to learn." List that as a strength, and add that she asks intelligent, germane questions and that you are impressed when she asks for reading material on a certain issue. This kind of specific feedback will encourage more of the same behavior.

WEAKNESSES

Take special care when you write down the employee's weak areas. Be as objective and as specific as possible. You are more likely to effect positive change and are less likely to engender defensiveness. Any area in which your employee receives a rating of less than 5 should be considered a weak area that needs improvement. You will want to concentrate, however, on areas that are most relevant to the person's job and to maintaining a pleasant work environment. If your kennel assistant has poor phone skills, you can have her not use the phone. However, if your kennel assistant has poor animal-handling skills, she is at risk for injury to herself and her charges.

List the weaknesses in order of their importance. Start with the area in which you would like the employee to improve first. If you have a new or inexperienced employee who has many areas in which she needs to improve, list only the ones that are most critical to her position. If you list too many items for improvement—more than three—your employee will be overwhelmed and disheartened. Let some areas wait for the next review. You may find that as she improves in the more important areas, the other attributes will improve as well.

FOR BEST RESULTS

Comments

Once again, be objective and specific. The comments that your employees make along with their ratings are critical. You will have a more successful review when you can be clear. For example, say your technician, Tara, has been given a satisfactory rating for her technical knowledge but is poorly rated for her desire to learn. You are naturally concerned, because you want to maintain a cutting-edge practice but cannot do that with technicians who will not continue to develop their skills. In the review, Tara disagrees with the assessment, but you are able to point out that your records show she has missed half the voluntary training sessions you set up for your staff in the past year. You also know from your financial records that Tara has not taken advantage of her continuing-education allowance in the past year. In addition, your other technician commented that she offered to train Tara on your new blood-pressure monitor twice, but Tara put her off both times. It is now difficult for Tara not to take your position seriously and reconsider her behavior to improve her performance.

What do you do with the employee who rates highly in almost every area? There are still areas in which she can improve—and this is an employee who is going to *want* to work on her skills and performance until she gets all 10s. If you have a receptionist who rates an 8 in phone manners, you are not likely to have any negative comments or constructive criticism from your staff to help in this area. Still, there must be some changes she could make to move from an 8 to a 9. You need to brainstorm with her without giving the appearance that her performance is in any way unsatisfactory. Maybe she needs to work on closing calls with overly chatty clients. Perhaps she is still passing off difficult clients to the office manager. These are skills she can work on.

SUMMARY

When performing world reviews, it is critical to provide training for all staff members so that everyone is comfortable with the process and with what is being asked of them. Evaluate all employees using the same criteria on a scale of 1 to 10, where 10 is the perfect all-around employee. Additionally, have veterinarians and managers evaluated on their special job functions by their supervisors or colleagues (not subordinates). Evaluate the employee's abilities in each component of each criterion before coming up with a rating. In addition to the numerical rating, provide specific examples of job performance for each criterion to back up your rating. Compile the ratings from all evaluators for each employee, and fill out a summary review sheet. Complete your evaluation by assessing last year's goals as well as the employee's strengths and weaknesses.

CHAPTER 8

GOAL SETTING

You are now approaching the final step in preparing for the review. One of the important components in the review process is identifying areas for improvement. Whether you are reviewing a substandard employee or a good employee, you should be able to identify areas to be improved. You are now going to translate these areas for improvement into specific goals for the employee. This is the part of the review that will carry through until the next review. Ask, "What would you like this employee to accomplish between now and then?"

BARE ESSENTIAL

Too often, this critical step is neglected. In all my years of work and through many performance reviews, only once were goals set as part of the review. Although it was difficult to focus on specific goals I wanted to achieve as a veterinarian in the next twelve months, setting goals helped me analyze what I wanted, expected, and hoped for from my job. When I heard my boss's goals for me, I learned much more about areas in which he wanted me to grow and the direction in which the practice was moving. Most of all, I knew precisely what was expected of me during the next twelve months and how my progress would be evaluated.

EXPERIENCE TALKING

GOALS TO CORRECT DEFICIENCIES

Similarly, you are going to set specific goals that will identify your expectations of your employee, enhance your employee's performance, and contribute to your practice. The priority goals—the ones that the employee must attain first—will be based on areas of deficiency. Therefore, based on the review, you must first identify any performance changes the employee must make in order to keep her job. If an employee is truly deficient, be clear on necessary improvements and what the outcome will be if she does not meet her goals. A receptionist who becomes aggressive with aggressive clients may be told that she needs to maintain her composure. A kennel assistant must learn to give medications to her charges and recognize the symptoms of bloat. A veterinarian must complete records by the end of the day. *Your goals should be that specific.* You must also decide what the consequence of inaction will be and advise your employee of that as well. The goals you set for a stellar employee will focus on enhancing current successes as well as on helping her understand your plans for your practice.

BARE ESSENTIAL

GOALS FOR THE PRACTICE

Having addressed any deficiencies, your next step is to set goals based on your plans for your practice. If you are purchasing a new dental unit, your technician will need to learn how to use it. If you want to increase inventory turnover, your inventory manager will need to develop a new system. If you would like to implement a geriatric program, you will need to provide additional training for all staff members: the receptionist and exam-room assistant will learn how to present the program, the technician will need to know what data to collect or what tests to run, and the veterinarian must be prepared to address the results of diagnostic tests and help educate clients about geriatric conditions.

Personal Goals

You now have a list of goals—hopefully two to five—that you would like to discuss at the review with your employee. Do not consider the list complete until you can include your employee's goals as well. She may have professional or personal goals that she is looking forward to meeting over the next year. Her goals will help you identify what her motivators are and how committed she is to your practice. They will show you how this employee believes she can maximize her potential for your practice. If your employee is studying to be an engineer, it is not likely that she will have a long-term commitment to your practice. If her goal is to spend more time with her children, you know her priorities and can decide if there is a way you can both get what you want. Having honest interest in *her* goals will help bond her to your practice.

Sometimes your employee's goals will also require a commitment on your part. For example, if an employee's goal is to be a Girl Scout troop leader for her daughter's troop, you may need to arrange for her to leave work at 3 P.M. one day a week and have the occasional Saturday off. Accommodating her should get you a happier, more dedicated employee. Perhaps an employee wants to pursue continuing education in a specific area like homeopathy. If you are not going to include that discipline in your practice, you may not see any benefit in sending her for the continuing education. At least you are now aware of your employee's interest and can decide if you are at risk of losing her to a practice that shares her interests. Consider whether you should send her for the training for her own benefit with the understanding she will not be able to use the knowledge at your practice.

When you are setting goals, remember to *be specific*! Do *not* set a goal of "computer skills;" set specific goals like "Learn how to run monthly reports" and "Be able to invoice every client without error or assistance." Also, set a time frame in which the goal should be reached. Give a reasonable time for the task. The goal "Always be on time" should be accomplished tomorrow. A goal to "Attend continuing education to learn about nutritional therapy" may take a year. You will not be able to monitor your employee's progress unless you have agreed to a time guideline. The goal may never even be reached without a set time frame. How many accomplishments can you think of in your life that were realized because of an impending deadline?

If a goal you set encompasses a broad area or will take longer than the time between now and the next review, break down the goal into smaller, manageable steps with shorter time frames. You may want a new employee to be proficient in computer operations in three months. That can be achieved in steps: entering new data, invoicing clients, printing reports, etc. Each step, then, should have its own time frame.

SUMMARY

Goal setting is a critical piece of the review process. The goals set for your employees should be based on their deficiencies, on your plans for your practice, and on the employees' personal goals. Any goal that is set should be defined specifically and given a concrete time frame in which the employee should achieve it.

CHAPTER 9

THE REVIEW MEETING

The appointed time has arrived and you are well prepared. Your employee is on her way down the hall toward your office. This chapter offers advice on how best to discuss the evaluation with your employee—from ratings to reprimands, from goal setting to salary changes. This chapter will help you better understand how to use the evaluation to improve both your work relationship with the employee and the employee's performance.

PRELIMINARIES

Before you even start, make the situation as comfortable as possible for yourself and your staff. There's no need to add to the tension that surrounds a review. Offer a beverage, begin with some banter, and step out from behind your desk if it will ease the tension. Although you want to get down to the business of the meeting, you also want to establish a climate that is friendly and open. Having said that, if a review will involve disciplinary action or a performance warning, maintain some formality to impress upon your employee the gravity of your words.

Many reviewees will feel most comfortable on neutral ground. You might consider holding the review meeting in a comfortable exam room or a meeting room instead of in your office (presuming privacy can be ensured). An alternative, particularly for self-conscious or uneasy reviewees, is to conduct the meeting off-site, perhaps over lunch. An extra consideration off-site is that your conversation won't be overheard by clients or others associated with your practice.

Each review should take forty-five to sixty minutes. Less time is needed if this is a follow-up review or a one- or three-month review for a new employee.

It can be especially difficult to rate a peer, specifically a veterinarian. If you are a manager rating a veterinarian, you are already at a disadvantage because you cannot fully evaluate the doctor's medical and surgical skills. A veterinarian can certainly evaluate those skills but must sometimes walk a fine line to avoid disrupting a collegial relationship. There is no magical way to address, when necessary, a colleague's faults. You should finesse your conversational style to smooth the conversation and should take a "we're in this together" approach. Follow the guidelines offered in this chapter. One positive result of this process is that you are likely to have a more personal, in-depth relationship with a colleague.

In any review, you need to outline the purpose of the review and the ground rules. "Tara, we're going to discuss several things. We're going to review your job performance over the past year. We'll go through the evaluation forms we've filled out, and then we'll talk about some objectives for the upcoming months. I'm sure you have some things that you would like to discuss with me as well. You may want to wait until I am finished summarizing your appraisal so we can have some perspective on the overall picture. I've put a lot of thought into your review and hope that you carefully consider my comments." Some managers would prefer to have the employee bring up any comments or goals at any time during the review. Other managers want to be sure that they have been able to paint the broad picture before an employee might dissect comments. You will have to decide how much back-and-forth interaction is appropriate at each step of the review discussion.

If it has not been given to you previously, take the employee's self-evaluation form. In fact, it is advisable to ask the reviewee to return the self-evaluation form at least a day in advance of the meeting. I recommend rescheduling the review if the employee has not completed the form. The self-evaluation form is the best way to get your employee's perspective about her performance and her relationship with the rest of the staff. By completing the form, she has also prepared for the review and for a discussion of objectives for the upcoming year.

BARE ESSENTIAL

Look through the self-evaluation form and quickly compare the employee's ratings to yours. (When I say "yours," I mean yours for a traditional review, or the staffs' for a world review.) Make special note of any markedly disparate areas. You will want to discuss these as you are going through the review form.

THE RATINGS

Guide the employee step by step through your review form and ratings. Discuss each item on the review form, one by one. You might gloss over areas that are not critical to her position or areas in which she rates well but not superbly. You will want to concentrate on areas that are most relevant to her job, where improvement is required, and where she truly excels. Do not just give the employee a number. Let her know what each rating means in terms of how well she is doing her job *in terms of what is expected of her.*

TIP

Give specific examples of her performance as it relates to each rating. "Tara, you received a strong rating of 7 for your product knowledge because the rest of the staff sees that you have in-depth knowledge to pass on to clients. Your coworkers feel they

FOR BEST RESULTS

A PRACTICAL GUIDE TO PERFORMANCE APPRAISALS

can come to you for an answer when they have a question. My job is easier because I know you advise our clients about possible side effects of the medication you dispense."

"Melissa, you received a poor rating for 'does not avoid any aspect of job' because you refuse to clean up accidents in the waiting room. Although it is an unpleasant task, it is a necessary one to maintain a pleasant and sanitary hospital. It isn't acceptable for you to avoid this part of your job."

I had a part-time employee who also had a full-time job elsewhere, yet worked at the hospital because she enjoyed it. She was an excellent employee with many fine attributes, but her knowledge base was poor. Although I would have loved for her to expand her knowledge base, that goal was practical only on a limited scale. Yet, she could continue to be a great part-time receptionist without it. Therefore, although her marks in this area were low, she knew from our discussion that I was not concerned about the ratings. Your employees need your guidance to put the evaluation in perspective.

When the employee's rating is markedly different from the average rating in an area, take a moment to figure out why. Is that area a problem for the employee? Is it clear she doesn't understand how or why her performance is lacking in this area? Are you using a different standard than your employee is using to evaluate performance? On average, supervisors and employees have 75 percent agreement on what the job responsibilities are. Your employee may legitimately perceive a different standard for her job than you do. Does the employee believe that you do not notice her strengths in this area? By bringing up the disparity, you will initiate a dialogue. Ask for the employee's reaction and listen carefully to your employee's viewpoint. Discuss any significant disparity until the two of you are on the same wavelength regarding the actual expectation for her job and whether she meets that expectation. Quickly summarize the point at the end.

Some employees are so successful at their jobs that you may feel you have little to discuss, and the review is basically a big pat

THE REVIEW MEETING

on the back. There are three points to remember regarding these super employees. First, you need to reward and affirm all the good work they do to encourage its continuance. Second, you need to be sure these employees do not focus on any truly minor problem areas. Finally, there is always room for improvement. Without making the employee feel that her performance is in any way inadequate, seek finer points that can still be tuned.

PERFORMANCE PROBLEMS

In contrast, it can be difficult to discuss problems in performance. If you were recently annoyed or angered by this employee's behavior, you may feel tempted to express your displeasure. When you actually sit down with the employee, however, your compassionate nature wants to minimize the trauma. Neither reaction is productive. You cannot be afraid to discuss the real issues. Unless you discuss the problem with an appropriate amount of emphasis, you are not giving your employee the opportunity to grow, nor will your practice benefit.

When you must discuss a problem area with an employee, be careful to criticize the behavior that is the problem, and not the person. Describe the problematic behavior. Give specific examples of when you or the staff have noticed this behavior. For example, "Diana, when you don't restock the exam room at the end of the day, we lose time out of a busy morning running to find items and seem disorganized to our clients."

If you are discussing an isolated incident, take the position that the employee has simply made a mistake. You are trying to find out the cause of the mistake so that it can be rectified. You want to show that you are helping the employee correct mistakes and work on weaker areas. You do *not* want to appear to dominate the employee. "Diana, exam room one didn't get restocked last night. Could you please take care of that now and doublecheck it

105

tonight for me?" Or, you might say, "Did something come up last night? It doesn't look like exam room one got restocked."

To keep a situation from becoming personal:

- Stick to comments about the behavior, not the person. Instead of saying, "You are a negative person," say, "When you roll your eyes and cross your arms in staff meetings, it appears you have a negative attitude." Instead of saying, "You always mess that up," say, "It appears that you are having trouble completing the lab tests properly."
- Use objective, factual statements: "The reminders were late going out three months straight." "I have received two client complaints about your phone manner." "We almost lost a patient when you gave it the wrong medication."
- Make comments related only to the job; do not bring up personal issues.
- Give specific examples: "Yesterday, I noticed that you let the phone ring five times before answering it because you were finishing up a personal conversation with another employee." "The surgery log isn't updated on the day you do surgery."
- Avoid absolutes. Instead of saying, "You are never on time for your shift," say, "You were late for work Monday, Tuesday, and Thursday." Instead of saying, "You always run late with appointments," say, "I have noticed that you sometimes get behind in your appointment schedule."

BARE ESSENTIAL

When you have identified a problem area and have used specific work examples to back you up, explain why it is a problem. Discuss the policy or philosophy you are enforcing. "Nancy, when you do not answer the phone on the first or second ring, clients may feel that we are too busy for them or that we are inefficient. They may even hang up rather than wait for us." "Linda, when you do not administer the preoperative sedative at the appropriate time, patients may need additional anesthesia and you may throw off our surgery schedule. If our surgery schedule shifts, we lose valuable time for more clients and more procedures."

Resolve any disagreements. Work on only one at a time. State the disagreement, your position, and the employee's position. Ask questions. Listen to your employee. Bring the disagreement to a conclusion. For example, say your biggest problem with an employee is her punctuality. Sometimes she is five minutes late for her shift, sometimes fifteen. It irks you and interferes with the efficiency of your practice. You are also worried about the message it sends to the rest of the staff because you have allowed it to continue this long. Your employee does not see the problem. She works very hard when she is at the practice and has many nonwork-related responsibilities. She has an excuse for every time she is late—the school bus was late, traffic was bad, or she got a phone call as she was walking out the door.

You might approach the conversation like this: "You and I disagree on the importance of punctuality. I believe that it is critical to the morale and efficiency of this practice that every single employee is on time for every shift. You believe you should receive leeway to accommodate personal issues. How can you accommodate the pressures of your morning and still get here on time to start your shift?" Your employee may be able to come up with some suggestions. If she cannot, you might suggest a change in her schedule. You must be absolutely clear, however, that tardiness is a behavior that will not be tolerated. This employee needs to understand how her tardiness impacts the rest of the staff and the hospital and what the penalties will be if her tardiness continues. Disciplinary action for problem behaviors is covered in Chapter Ten.

GENERAL TIPS

Do not argue with the employee. An employee certainly should let you know about any extenuating circumstances that you are not aware of, and she should clarify misunderstandings. That doesn't mean she should argue with the review. If you find the conversation becoming a debate, you might sit back and say, "We have different perspectives on this issue. I don't want to debate what has happened in the past. I want to be sure of how things are going to be handled in the future. This is what I need to happen . . ." and then describe an appropriate resolution to the problem or the proper way for the employee to handle the problem situation. If your hospital does world reviews, it is harder for the employee to argue against her evaluation. It is a lot harder to argue that the perspectives of six people are wrong.

You also want your employees to have an accurate perspective of the importance of your comments. Some employees will downplay your stated concerns. Others will dwell on one comment or area that you find relatively insignificant or will negate the positive review you have given them because of the one area you have marked for improvement over the next year. It is important that you finish the rating section of the review by advising your employee which points are the most pertinent—which have the highest priority.

Four more tips to get you through the review:

1. **Stay focused.** It is easy to get off track during your conversation. If you allow the conversation to wander, not only do you waste time you need for the review, you also devalue the importance of the information you are discussing. If you find yourself starting to get off track, bring the discussion back to the review by saying something like, "We've sure moved away from the subject. I'd like to talk with you more about this some other time, but I don't want to run out of time now for the evaluation. We were talking about . . ." or, "I'm going to interrupt you here because I'm concerned we've wandered too far off the topic. Let's get back to . . ." If the employee continues to draw the conversation away from the review, she may be showing that

THE REVIEW MEETING

she is uncomfortable being evaluated or that she may be afraid of what's coming. Let her know that there are many positive points you want to make about her performance and about her future with the practice, and therefore you would like her to give you time to make some comments before you discuss them with her. Once you have covered a group of points, you can then draw her back into a discussion.

2. **Do not permit your employees to belabor minor points.** You do not want to waste this valuable meeting debating a relatively inconsequential rating or comment when there are bigger points to get through. If your employee seems hung up, summarize the point, put it in context of the complete review, and let the employee know you are moving on to another topic. By the same token, you must not dwell on past history or on isolated incidents. If the employee had a deficiency nine months ago that has now been corrected, the only pertinent piece of information is the correction. Incidents should be discussed only as specific data to show patterns of behavior. Unless an incident is so horrible—stealing or cursing at a client, for example—the incident itself should not be the focus. The focus should be its relevance to a behavior you want to see improved. Do not argue the fine points of the incident itself; discuss the general behavior that warrants improvement.

3. **Do not compare.** Your employee's performance is being judged against the standard for her job or against the "ideal" employee for traditional and world reviews, respectively. She is not being judged against your other employees. Please do not direct your employee to be more like another staff member, and do not imply that she needs to be more like you. You also do not want to comment that an employee is better than your other employees. Confine your discussion to work-related behaviors, not comparisons. Comparing staff members establishes the wrong standard by which employees are rated

and sets up bad feelings and competition among employees. Along these same lines, avoid saying, "If I were you . . ." Telling an employee how you would handle a situation in her shoes can cause "Well, you're not me" type resentment and can prevent an employee from solving the problem for herself.

4. **Do not solve an employee's problems for her.** This is true of both personal and professional problems. You are not there to play therapist. If an employee brings up a personal problem that is affecting her attitude or work, ask questions to direct the conversation back to work. For example, if your employee cannot attend an off-site training meeting that you feel is important and begins to give you a list of reasons why, you might say, "If you can't attend this meeting, I would like you to think of a way to get the same training that *will* fit your schedule." You then make it clear you are not interested in discussing the ins and outs of her personal schedule or hindrances, only in how the work will be accomplished and how performance will be enhanced.

Sometimes, an employee will bring up personal issues during a review even when they are not directly related to your comments. If you are not interested in listening to personal issues, let her know the focus will be kept on business. "Katie, I appreciate that might be a difficult situation for you. Right now, we need to concentrate on the review."

Now, what if the problem is a professional one? You do not want to try to solve that one either. You want your employees to be problem solvers. Perhaps you have identified an employee's lack of initiative as a problem. You might say to the employee, "There are times when business is slow and I haven't seen you find work to do. Can you think of some things you could be doing during the slower times?" Hopefully, your employee will be able to come up with a couple of ideas. Write them down on the review sheet. Continue, "Those seem like good ideas. You might also want to keep in mind . . ." If your employee is unable to think of productive work (after all, the problem *is* lack of initiative), you might go halfway toward solving the problem. You might tell her that you will make a list of occasional or extra tasks that need to be done. Your employee can refer to the list whenever she has a free moment for other work.

GOAL SETTING

Goal setting is a great way to energize your employee at the end of the review. Setting goals gets your employee to think forward and to plan for better things for herself and for your practice. It emphasizes your commitment to each other.

When you prepared for the review, you already decided on the goals you want this employee to meet (see Chapter Eight). You chose these goals based on weak areas the employee needs to develop and on the future needs of your practice. When you discuss with your employee the goals you have set, give her a chance to decide how best to achieve them. Some are obvious. If one of your goals for a receptionist is for her to attend a training meeting offered in a nearby city in March, there isn't much left to decide. However, if one of your goals is for your receptionist to improve her telephone skills, let her list three ways in which she believes she can do that. If she is having difficulty, you can certainly jog the conversation. You can ask her to compile a list, within the week, of three steps she can take to accomplish that goal. Here is an example of how your conversation might proceed.

> "Sarah, one of the goals I set for you based on this performance review is to improve your telephone skills. Have you given any thought to how you might be able to improve this skill?"
>
> "No, I really haven't."
>
> "In general, what techniques could a receptionist use to do that part of her job better?"
>
> "Well, maybe there's some sort of course that helps tell you what to say on the phone."

"That's a good idea. It seems we get seminar brochures here at the hospital all the time. I'll dig through some in my desk and see if I can find one on telephone techniques. If I can't, why don't you make some calls and see if one of the veterinary organizations offers that kind of training. They might even have tapes. It also might help to have somebody listen to some of your calls and tell you how you might say things better. Is there somebody you work with who has really good phone skills and who you would be comfortable having as a mentor in this area?"

"Mary and I get along really well and I think she has good phone skills."

"Great. Why don't you talk to Mary and see if she is up for giving you some feedback."

Make sure your employee is invested in the goals you have set. She must understand why you have set them and how they are important to the best, most efficient operation of your hospital. If she doesn't make the goal her own, you decrease the chance she will achieve it.

Add goals that your employee would like to achieve. Hopefully, she has come into the review with some ideas of what she would like to accomplish over the next year. She has already invested in these, so try to make them happen. You may, however, have to sort through the list. You want to be sure that you have not set too many goals. You will lose sight of some and will risk having an employee be spread too thin or risk running out of time to achieve them. You want your employees to be pushed and challenged. You also want to make sure that all the goals you set are attainable in the time period you set up. If the list seems too long, agree together which goals will take priority and which should be met only after the priorities.

Finally, determine if there are goals *you* need to meet in relation to the employee. Sometimes, work will be necessary for you after the review, not just for the employee. Your work may be as simple as tracking down information. It may be as complicated as

THE REVIEW MEETING

setting up a new training program requested by the staff. Make sure you are maximizing your relationship by meeting your obligations to your staff.

SUMMARIZE THE REVIEW

Your employee wants several questions to be answered at this point:

- Overall, how am I doing?
- How can I improve my skills?
- Should I expect any business changes that may affect my job?
- Is there an opportunity for advancement?

During your summary, do not revisit minor points. Summarize the areas in which the employee does very well. Bring up the areas that need improvement and agree on a plan for those improvements. Quickly review the goals you have established. If there are any major business changes you anticipate that have not already been discussed, bring those up as well.

Ensure that the employee has a clear understanding of the evaluation. Ask if she has any remaining questions. Be sure you have written down any agreements you have made. Check that the goals you have set are specific and clear to the employee. Have you obtained the employee's commitment to the goals? If you haven't, you are not finished yet.

BARRIERS TO EFFECTIVE COMMUNICATION

For a truly constructive review, there must be open communication and mutual goals. You must count on your employees to respond professionally and honestly. Sometimes, there are barriers to effective communication. The barriers may stem from the employee's personality, from the employee's relationship with you, or from the work environment itself.

Some individuals think reviews are unnecessary and refuse to participate or put stock in the evaluation. These people believe they have nothing to learn from the person(s) evaluating them. Fortunately, these individuals are few and far between in veterinary practices. If you do have an employee who exhibits this predisposition, you must force participation in the review. The first step is for the employee to complete the self-review. The self-evaluation ensures involvement. The next step is to discuss significant points of the review and guide the employee to find solutions.

Some employees are too intimidated—by you or by the process—to ask for or give real feedback. These employees will "yes" you to death. They will simply follow along and implicitly or verbally agree with everything you say. With these employees, it is especially important to conduct the review in an informal, relaxed environment. Let them know that you feel the only way to have a productive performance evaluation is to hear how they feel about their own work. Fortunately, you will have the self-evaluation to help you understand what this employee thinks. This is one of the reasons why I recommend you always have the self-evaluation form when conducting a performance appraisal. This employee is not going to want to complete a self-evaluation and risk a "confrontation" based on differences from your ratings.

Another barrier to effective feedback is specifically related to the culture you create at your hospital. Employees will not actively participate in the review process if they believe feedback flows only in one direction. Employees will hold this belief only if prior experience tells them this is so. Therefore, if the management at your practice is accustomed to solving problems, giving instructions, and providing training without any input from the staff or without encouraging their feedback, you cannot expect them to suddenly start speaking up in the review.

THE REVIEW MEETING

Another barrier to effectiveness is blandness. Be clear. Do not reduce the importance of poor ratings. You may be uncomfortable doling out a poor rating and may want to protect your employee's feelings. Remember that you are not helping the employee *or* your practice if you are not honest and objective.

Give your employee the good and the bad. Do not make small issues seem bigger than they are. Be clear on the importance of each rating so that it does not overemphasize other areas.

HOW PERSONALITY TRAITS AFFECT THE REVIEW

Personality traits may affect your employee's participation in her review. Recognizing these traits in an employee allows you to work out a game plan beforehand. For example, an employee who lacks self-confidence will be focused on saying what she believes you want to hear. She won't trust her own opinions and assessments. She will be most comfortable parroting yours. The best strategy with this employee (beyond the self-evaluation) is to ask for her thoughts before you give yours. If her reply is nonspecific or hesitant, ask questions to bring out her opinion.

A self-centered employee, on the other hand, will not listen to your needs. This employee is likely to look forward to the review more than the average employee because she will be the focus of your attention. A self-centered employee only wants to know how changes will affect her and how her needs can be accommodated. This employee is likely to rate poorly in team skills. Your best chance for a turnaround in team skills, and for her to enhance her performance, is to explain how achieving the practice's goals will positively influence her. For example, as the practice's income grows, more money will be available for salaries. If she starts taking on special projects, she will more likely be considered for advancement.

Employees who are strictly task-oriented may be unable to see the big picture. Some employees can't get beyond their daily duties. They have little comprehension of the structure and rationale behind the daily grind. When you are evaluating such an employee, keep the conversation at her level. It may not help to explain why you have a change in policy or why she needs to learn a new procedure. It is best to give specific, basic instructions, such as, "Starting on January 1, you need to be ready to use the new computer system. There will be a training program on December 15 for you to attend." Or, "Instead of using telazol to anesthetize cats for neuters, we are going to start using ketamine and Valium. Here are the dosages I want you to memorize and start using."

An employee lacking integrity will have an inflated view of herself and of her role in the practice. She will think that any changes that have to be made should be made not by her but by you and other staff members. This is not a desirable employee. If this employee has not already shown her true colors, she tends to do so in her first review. This employee will give herself higher ratings than the rest of the staff gives her. She will argue with you about why her opinion is more correct, and how the rest of the staff doesn't see or understand the situation. If you want to work with this employee, you may have to speak to her forcefully and directly. For example, "I understand that your perception is different and that it is difficult for you to accept this evaluation. You must understand that these ratings are meaningful. I take them very seriously. I am telling you that you must improve in these areas if you would like to keep your position here. Here is a list of the things I need to see improvement in."

Addressing Emotional Responses

The anxiety associated with a review can bring out the worst in some people. Some employees come in ready for a fight. Others are intimidated and afraid. Some will cry because of their jangled nerves. Most of your employees will be calm and professional, but you should anticipate any of the following responses.

The Crier

Anxiety, anger, or intimidation can result in a strong enough emotional reaction to elicit crying. Your employee is likely to be embarrassed if she cries. Offer her a tissue and say something like, "All the anticipation really builds up, doesn't it?" Let her know that you understand her reaction. Say that you'd like to continue with the review. If she needs some time to collect herself, allow her to do so. If she agrees to continue, completely ignore any sniffling or crying from that point onward. You will only embarrass her and disrupt a vital conversation. Your conversation will have less weight if it is often interrupted with, "Are you sure you are all right?" and, "We can take a break if you need to."

The Volcano

Even small comments can agitate this employee; a significant problem may tempt her to end the discussion by leaving the review. Do not back down on your comments simply because your employee is showing an extreme and undesirable reaction. If her anger is getting the best of her, she may say things she will later regret. If she makes an angry comment, you might say to her, "I can see that this review is bringing out some strong emotions. We still need to complete the review. You may want to wait until it is over and think about everything I've said before you comment so that you can see the whole picture."

If the employee attempts to leave the review before it is done, you need to bring her back. Before she has a chance to walk out, let her know that leaving the review is not an option. Tell her that you can see she has strong feelings about what you are saying. Invite her to retake a seat and collect herself while you do a few minutes of paperwork. An alternative to this strategy is to allow the reviewee to remain in the room while you leave for a few minutes. When you are ready to start again, set another ground rule. Even if she is angry, she needs to hear the entire evaluation. If she doesn't feel she can make productive comments, then she is welcome to follow up with comments within a week following the evaluation.

The Clam

The clam has a physical reaction to her anxiety over the review. This may manifest as clammy hands, sweating, headaches, or nausea. You may see complexion changes. You need to do your best to put the clam at ease. Set up a comfortable environment and take some time to have a benign conversation to break the ice. Start the review discussion with comments about the practice's year and future plans or with this employee's successes.

The Silent Sufferer

This employee internalizes her emotional reaction so that you do not see any of the effects. She seems unnaturally withdrawn and quiet. She is too fearful or anxious of you, of the review, or of her emotions to participate. Ask open-ended questions and use her self-evaluation to draw her out.

SALARY CHANGES

Ideally, salary would never be discussed during a performance review. If your employee is going to learn her new pay rate at the time of the review, she is going to be most interested in the two minutes of the review when she learns what that rate is. Much of her reaction to the review will actually be based on the pay. A low or modest pay change will negate all the positive ideas you discussed, and any pay increase will negate significant problems you stressed.

The way to avoid this problem is to stop tying pay to the review. For example, consider giving an annual inflation/cost-of-living increase that all employees receive on the same date. Your employees will see that you understand the importance of maintaining the

THE REVIEW MEETING

same true income level. They see that you raise prices yearly in accordance with increased costs and that those changes affect them.

There are two problems with a cost-of-living adjustment. First, you must ensure that your employees or a court does not perceive it as a merit raise. You do not want to give the appearance that you are rewarding poor performers with additional wages. Second, employees may come to see this as an entitled raise even when it is well defined. In a noninflationary period, they will be disappointed when they receive no adjustment.

Base any other salary increases on established performance goals. The pay is changed as goals are met. Some companies adjust salaries two months after the review to respond to performance changes based on the review discussion.

If you are conducting a world review, it makes sense to use the data you gather to affect any bonus that may be distributed among your staff. You want to reward employees who most affect the success of your practice. Part of the contribution may simply be the number of hours each staff member contributes to the practice. The other part of the contribution is the technical, team, and client-relation skills each employee brings. Your review assesses each employee's level of expertise in these areas and gives you a numerical value with which to work. Those two number sets—hours worked and skills and knowledge base—can be used as a basis to formulate a rewards program.

If it is your practice to tie salary to the review, then get it out of the way at the beginning of the review. Why leave the employee in suspense? Let her know what raise she is getting and whether it is merely a cost-of-living adjustment, a moderate increase, or a significant increase. If you do not add that simple comment, your employee is left to wonder how much you are trying to reward her and may resort to grilling other employees about their increases. Then, continue with the review to explain how her performance has been evaluated to culminate in that pay change.

You may have an added dimension to the review if your employee attempts to negotiate her pay. She may negotiate by mentioning skills that she believes increase her value to you or by discussing market pay ranges. Be prepared to counter. You should know the market rate for employees in your area. If you have given her a raise that you truly believe rewards her for her contributions to your practice, you are not likely to have much room for changing your number. Negotiating salary once also sets you up for a salary battle at each review.

If your employee has valid reasons why her pay should be higher and you can afford the additional pay, accommodate her request. If you believe the pay you are offering is fair and adequate for her skills, do not negotiate. Instead of debating the number you are offering today, let her know what goals she will need to meet in order to receive a higher salary.

EVALUATING THE EVALUATION

If a performance appraisal does not go as well as you hoped, remember that humans are not always a predictable lot. Use each review as a lesson. If the review goes well, ask yourself why.

- Was it because you already had a particularly amiable relationship with that staff person?
- Was it because the review was largely positive?
- Was it because you were prepared to handle the rough spots and got through them okay?

Whatever the reason, create an environment in which you can repeat that good performance.

When a review does not go as well, evaluate the reasons.

- Did the review take twice as long as you had expected because you chatted too much or because your employee had difficulty accepting those weak spots you want her to work on?

- Did your employee get emotional, perhaps even begin to cry, and make you uncomfortable?
- Did your employee argue with you, and you found yourself arguing back despite your best intentions not to?

Any problem with a review can be fixed. Decide how you would handle the same situation differently the next time. When it arises again, you will handle it better.

SUMMARY

Your discussion during the evaluation needs to provide balance and direction. As you take your employee through each criterion and discuss her performance, you should be building a picture of her work throughout the review period based on objective data and specific examples. Reward successes. Address failures. End the review by building on the information to establish new objectives.

Each employee will have a different reaction to the process. Adjust your comments to accommodate this difference to ensure the best outcome. Even when you do not feel the review has gone well, you and the employee both will have learned something from the process.

CHAPTER 10

DISCIPLINARY ACTION AND LEGAL ISSUES

Disciplinary action is an unfortunate yet inevitable duty of any practice owner or manager. You are fortunate indeed if you have never had an employee whose substandard performance or improper behavior demanded action. This chapter discusses behaviors that warrant disciplinary action and appropriate steps to take in response to those behaviors.

Many employment-law issues are beyond the scope of this book, including pregnancy discrimination and resignation, because those situations are not related to performance appraisals. This chapter concentrates on the areas of employment law that are specifically related to employee performance and termination. The information will help you evaluate whether your actions in a review, disciplinary process, or termination would help you in a termination-related court case. You will also learn about peripheral areas related to termination so that you can increase your odds of not ending up in court with a terminated employee. When you have a specific legal question about a situation in your hospital, contact your practice's lawyer or a lawyer who specializes in employment law.

BARE ESSENTIAL

THE PERFORMANCE APPRAISAL AS A LEGAL DOCUMENT

The performance appraisal can be an important legal document in a wrongful-termination or discrimination suit. It is your best, and often only, substantiation that an employee was terminated for substandard performance. To ensure that your decision to terminate a poor performer will be affirmed in any lawsuit, follow these guidelines in your review process.

- Give regular and timely reviews.
- Give specific examples of an employee's behavior to back up your assessment.
- Use formal evaluation criteria to limit subjective responses. The employee's job description and/or your mutually agreed-upon employee objectives for the review period should be the standards used when measuring your employee's performance. Gather data to validate your appraisal. (Some examples of data sources are given in Chapter Four.)
- Clearly define an employee's problem areas and outline possible solutions during the review. Include this information on the written evaluation. This will show that the employee was aware of performance problems and that you assisted in their resolution.
- Summarize the review, have the employee sign it, and place it in the employee's file. An employee who signs the review cannot later deny she was aware of the information. The employee may also provide a written response to any performance appraisal. The response must be placed in the employee's file.

You must ensure equitable treatment of all employees in the review process. It is a form of discrimination to hold different employees to different standards. Performing world reviews may give you an edge over using traditional reviews in the event of a lawsuit, because one manager or staff person's view will not unduly influence the appraisal. A world review shows a court that a poor assessment was not due to the prejudices of a single evaluator. The world review, done properly, also has fewer potential biases and thus promotes the most realistic appraisal. For accuracy of the review process, it is important to show that all raters have interaction with the rated employee, proving they have personal knowledge of her performance.

POLICIES AND PROCEDURES

For your performance appraisal, and any decisions to terminate based on the appraisal, to be seen as just, a court will look at more than the appraisal itself. A judge or arbitrator will also evaluate the rules and procedures you have established at your practice and whether you have followed them. And here begins one of the great conundrums of operating a business.

Having written guidelines and policies in place reduces the number of employee questions, and it provides a standard for day-to-day operations and a yardstick that can be used to your benefit in any lawsuit initiated by a terminated employee. Employees can simply refer to your policy on absenteeism or the timing of reviews to know what to expect. Policies also help to ensure that all employees are treated equitably and fairly. There is one preestablished answer to a question or problem, not a different answer depending on whom you ask.

Another advantage of written policies and procedures is that, when followed, they will support your actions in a lawsuit. If an employee has been informed of the rules, and the rules are legally acceptable, the employee will be held to them.

A business owner therefore might be inclined to write a book of policies and rules to outline a response to every situation and to counteract any potential legal or regulatory claim. (If staffing issues don't drive you mad, that surely would.) The problem with this scenario, aside from the time it requires, is that you cannot possibly anticipate all the situations that might arise in the course of business. Another problem is that your policies may come back to haunt you. A judge will look at whether your rules and policies have been applied consistently. You cannot fire one employee for chronic tardiness or cursing if you have allowed another employee to remain on staff following similar episodes.

You want the benefits of defined policies and procedures but not the potential headaches. Despite the fact that your policies cannot be all-inclusive, it is best to have them and continue to adjust them in response to new situations or information. The benefits outweigh the risks.

A sample of how you might write a section in your employee handbook on employee appraisals is given in Appendix 1 (page 145).

EMPLOYMENT-AT-WILL

From a legal standpoint, most employees are employees at-will. Employment at-will means that an employee can resign or can be terminated at any time, and for any reason, as long as it is not discriminatory.

CONTRACT EMPLOYEES

Most veterinary practices have veterinarians under contract. An employment contract should define a parting of the ways when that becomes necessary. At termination, the standard you are held to, then, is the standard that you have defined in your contract. If your contract defines that you may terminate your veterinary employee at-will, then you may do so. If your contract defines that you may only terminate for cause, you must be able to show cause.

Employment contracts may be written for either consideration. You might be able to fire at-will but may then be required to pay a defined severance package. If you are terminating for cause, typically the severance package is not given. What is important is that you follow the provisions of your signed contract.

PROTECTED CLASSES

The Civil Rights Act of 1964 prohibits the discharge of an employee because of race, color, sex, national origin, or religion. Sex includes pregnancy, childbirth, or related medical conditions. Age discrimination, referring to employees more than forty years of age, is prohibited under the Age Discrimination in Employment Act. Your former employee may use this protected class status as the basis of a lawsuit, however unfounded. Any such lawsuits should be prevented or minimized by adhering to the procedures discussed, including conducting proper performance reviews, having a progressive disciplinary policy, and advising the employee of the true reason for her termination.

The Occupational Safety and Health Act of 1970 offers "whistleblower" protection. The act prohibits the discharge of an employee for exercising her right to notify OSHA of a violation or participate in an OSHA investigation. The Americans with Disabilities Act of 1990 prohibits the discharge of an employee due to a legally protected disability.

These are federal protections that apply in every state. That does not mean, of course, that these employees cannot be terminated for poor performance or for outrageous conduct. It simply means that they cannot be terminated for their disability alone or in retaliation.

EXCEPTIONS TO EMPLOYMENT-AT-WILL DOCTRINE

The exceptions to the employment-at-will doctrine get a little trickier because they vary among states. First, five states maintain strict employment-at-will doctrines without adopting any exceptions. These states are Delaware, Florida, Georgia, Louisiana, and Mississippi. In these states, employees are truly at-will and can be terminated at any time for any reason as long as the reason is not discriminatory. At the opposite end of the spectrum is the state of Montana. Montana abandoned at-will employment in 1987 by adopting legislation that requires an arbitration system for a claim of wrongful discharge and rights of job reinstatement or financial compensation if the discharge is indeed unjustified. The following states, while not progressing to Montana's employment standard, have adopted all of the exceptions (see below) to employment at-will: Alaska, Arizona, California, Connecticut, Idaho, Massachusetts, and Nevada. These states are trending toward limiting an employer's right to termination to cases based solely on just and documented rationale.

Breach of An Implied Contract

For every rule, there is an exception. The breach-of-implied-contract exception clarifies that even if you advise employees that they are at-will, your procedures and documents may say otherwise and may thus create an implied contract. Wording in an employee handbook or on job applications, or your promise to follow certain procedures and policies, can justify a claim that you have forgone at-will employment.

The McGraw-Hill Company had a statement in its employee handbook that just and sufficient cause was required for termination. In the 1982 case of Weiner v. McGraw-Hill, the court rejected the company's claim that this statement in the personnel handbook was nonbinding. The company could not fire at-will.

Workers have been similarly successful in regaining jobs or winning cash awards in cases in which a manual represented that discharge would only be for cause or when progressive disciplinary procedures existed and were not followed. A Michigan Supreme Court found that an "employer's stated policies and established procedures" may create a "right to continued employment absent cause for discharge" that is "enforceable in contract."

In the 1980 cases of Toussaint *v.* Blue Cross and Blue Shield of Michigan and Ebling *v.* Masco Corp., the Michigan court ruled, "When a prospective employee inquires about job security and the employer agrees that the employee shall be employed as long as he does his job, a fair construction is that the employer has agreed to give up his right to discharge at-will without assigning cause and may only discharge for cause." The court may also discern implied obligations due to longevity of service, employment benefits that are dependent on continued service, such as stock options, or the sacrifice of another employment opportunity.

To avoid this type of wrongful-discharge claim, either emphasize that employment is at-will or establish a system of termination for cause only. If you wish to maintain true at-will employment, take care to avoid the terms "permanent," "probationary," or "tenure" in job advertisements, promotional brochures, and job applications. Avoid the term "probationary" because it implies permanent employment upon successful completion of the probationary period. Use the terms "introductory" or "trial" to refer to the "probationary" period. Train those who interview potential employees, review employees, or provide policy information to employees not to ensure permanent employment, training opportunities, or advancement. If you choose a policy of termination for cause only, dismissals must be in accordance with your established policies and procedures, be fair and equitable, and be applied consistently and uniformly.

Breach of Implied Covenant of Good Faith and Fair Dealing

An example that illustrates the breach of implied covenant of good faith and fair dealing is the case where a Massachusetts court found, "In every contract there exists an implied covenant of good faith and fair dealing," and then extrapolated this to the employer-employee relationship. In Fortune *v.* National Cash Register, the court found that the employer had acted in bad faith by discharging a sales associate so that the company would not have to pay a sales commission. The 1974 case of Monge v. Beebe Rubber Company was brought by an employee who was discharged after she refused to date her supervisor. In another case, the New Hampshire court found that, "A termination by the employer of a contract of employment-at-will which is motivated by bad faith or malice or is based on retaliation is not in the best interest of the economic system or the public good and constitutes a breach of the employment contract."

Violation of Public Policy

The public-policy exception relates primarily to retaliatory terminations. Public policy was first defined by the California court in the case of Safeway Stores v. Retail Clerks in 1953 as "that principle of law which holds no citizen can lawfully do that which has a tendency to be injurious to the public or against the public good." This has nothing to do with a contractual agreement for employment and everything to do with a terminated employee's right to bring civil action against a prior employer for a violation of a duty imposed by law.

One of the first cases to test the public-policy exception to at-will employment was Petermann v. Teamsters Local 396, before the California Appeals Court. A terminated employee won against his prior employer, who discharged him for refusing to commit perjury. In Illinois, the termination of a supervisor who informed police that a coworker was attempting to sell company merchandise for personal profit was found to be against public policy. Likewise, in Pennsylvania, a terminated employee prevailed who had been fired for refusing to support his employer's lobbying efforts to pass a bill in the state legislature. Other cases that have been upheld as against public policy involved retaliatory discharge for refusing to evade jury duty and refusing to engage in price fixing.

Several states have clarified the public-policy exception. The Illinois court noted in Palmatee v. International Harvester that "a matter must strike at the heart of a citizen's social rights, duties and responsibilities before the tort will be allowed." The Wisconsin court clarified that no employer is "subject to suit merely because a discharged employee's conduct was praiseworthy or because the public may have derived some benefit from it." Related to the public-policy exception, the following twenty-two states and the District of Columbia have specifically protected employees from retaliatory termination who file workers' compensation claims or who testify in a related proceeding: Alabama, Alaska, California, Delaware, District of Columbia, Florida, Hawaii, Illinois, Kentucky, Louisiana, Maryland, Massachusetts, Missouri, Nevada, New Jersey, New York, North Carolina, North Dakota, Ohio, Oklahoma, Oregon, Texas, and Virginia.

The last cause of action for wrongful discharge is a private-tort exception that includes punitive damages and damages for emotional distress in addition to economic damages. This is the least important grounds for exception to the employment-at-will doctrine. Generally, the plaintiff must demonstrate intentional conduct that was extreme and outrageous, causing the plaintiff to suffer severe emotional distress.

DISCIPLINARY ACTION

A review is not the only time that formal reprimands are appropriate. However, when you are doing a complete evaluation of an employee's work, a bad situation may present itself. Perhaps you hadn't realized that your weekend kennel assistant was late for every shift until you checked time cards in anticipation of the review. Perhaps you are only now learning of a receptionist's argument with a client, or that your technician is filling out safety reports with made-up information.

A PRACTICAL GUIDE TO PERFORMANCE APPRAISALS

REASONS TO DISCIPLINE

Every employer has the right to discipline and discharge problem employees, whether a problem shows up in a review or in the daily course of business. A number of situations, in addition to poor performance, justify this action, including:

- absenteeism
- inattention to health and safety
- insubordination
- dishonesty
- moonlighting at a competitor's practice
- discourtesy
- damage to company property
- substance abuse
- dress-code violations
- fighting
- sexual harassment
- certain off-duty conduct
- theft
- violence

Examples of specific actions that warrant discipline are when an employee slaps a pet or curses at a client, or when a moonlighting worker fraudulently uses sick leave. These actions clearly demand discipline. Other actions, such as insubordination, can fall into a gray area. When does an employee's inactivity become insubordination and justify discipline? If the employee understood your instructions, the order was in line with the employee's duties, and there is no reason for the employee to refuse your order and yet she has, the employee is being insubordinate.

Another gray area is off-duty misconduct. Here again, it is helpful to have a policy in place. An appropriate policy might be that any employee who is convicted of a misdemeanor or felony charge or is proven to have acted immorally (stealing or selling drugs,

BARE ESSENTIAL

for example) may be immediately dismissed. Off-duty misconduct always requires a complete investigation to ensure that your decision is based on *facts*. If you are unable to prove inappropriate off-the-job activities, your best recourse is to collect evidence of poor performance on the job.

If you wish to discipline someone you think is abusing alcohol, prescription drugs, or nonprescription drugs, or who is even drinking moderately during lunch breaks, be sure that you follow company policy precisely. These are always difficult situations for an employer and sometimes for the courts. Having a defined policy regarding substance abuse is a good start. Even then, if there is no witness to the alcohol or drug use, you must rely on random testing (if that is already part of your practice's policy) or concentrate solely on performance deficits without mention of the abuse.

Progressive Discipline

During any disciplinary action, keep in mind that the employee has certain rights that you must observe and respect in order to increase the probability of your winning any subsequent lawsuit instigated by a terminated employee. These rights include:

- the right to consistent and equitable responses to rules violations based on the facts of the incident; and
- the right to be informed of your expectations and rules and the consequences of not meeting those expectations.

Traditionally, a series of disciplinary steps, or progressive discipline, is taken with any action that does not demand immediate termination: verbal warning, written warning, final written warning, and termination. Among your practice procedures, you might fashion a progressive discipline policy to categorize your response to problems. Also develop appropriate responses to the most common forms of misconduct. This should ensure employee awareness and consistent treatment. Your entire staff will know how problems are handled and what they should expect when they make errors.

Once you have established, even informally, a progressive discipline policy, you must follow it. Respond to any action that does not demand immediate dismissal with an oral warning, a first written warning, and a final written warning. If you do not follow your own policy to terminate employment in accordance with this procedure, a discharged employee may have a claim for wrongful discharge. Courts have reinstated employees who were not given official notice that further violations would result in termination. Alternatively, having given a final warning, if you do not terminate an employee for an additional violation, your policy will be seriously undermined. The policy is meant to provide a framework for disciplinary action and ensure the equitable treatment of all employees. That the policy must be consistently applied is evidenced in the case of Goodwill *v.* Oklahoma Department of Corrections. An employee who had pleaded guilty to drug-possession charges was immediately fired in accordance with company policy. This employee successfully sued for front pay (a substitute remedy that offers payment of future earnings in lieu of reinstatement) and back pay as well as for emotional distress because he was able to prove that other employees with felony convictions had not been disciplined at all.

Verbal Warning

The first step at the onset of a behavioral problem is often a verbal warning. This typically means that you witnessed an unacceptable behavior and are advising the employee of it. This could be as simple as advising a doctor who took a file home not to do it again or correcting a kennel assistant who neglected to administer a medication to a kenneled dog. Whatever the problem, if you have to verbally correct or warn the employee, document the reprimand in writing in the employee's file. A written document that a verbal warning was given shows that procedures were followed, describes the nature of the problem, and indicates that corrective action was taken.

Written Warning

If the employee does not take corrective action, she is next given a written warning. Give a written warning whenever an employee performs in a manner that may ultimately warrant termination. The warning should:

- define the problem behavior or area(s) of substandard performance
- describe specific instances that illustrate the problem
- suggest ways to correct the problem
- provide a time frame in which the problem should be corrected
- describe the consequence of continued similar behavior

Typically, this written warning is discussed in private with the employee, and the employee is given a copy of the formal warning. The warning is also placed in the employee's file. If the substandard performance is identified in conjunction with a review, the warning should be appended to the review. Substandard performance warnings can be given at any time, however, without benefit of a formal evaluation.

Always follow these steps when you need to given an employee a written warning:

1. Get your facts straight. Be sure of the situation before you take any action. Have any documentation on hand. If other employees are witnesses to an event, have them write and sign a brief summary of what they saw for your records.
2. Document situations as they happen. Some problems are not large enough to warrant a reprimand when they are a one-

time event. However, a pattern of behavior might warrant a reprimand. When you witness events, make note of them. The episode may be tardiness or a poor attitude or a poorly handled client situation. If the single event is significant, or if you see a pattern of poor behavior, a reprimand is warranted. Your memory will not be fresh enough to document situations at a later date. You will also find it difficult to establish a pattern of behavior without notes.
3. Keep observations job related. Use objective criteria whenever you can—time cards, computer records, or fraudulent reports.
4. Criticize the undesirable behavior, not the person. Limit your observations to the problem as it relates to the employee's job performance or to the practice.
5 Avoid conclusions. Let the employee's actions speak for themselves.
6. Avoid emotion. If you are angry over an employee's actions, it is best to wait until you have cooled down before you discuss the problem with her. Some actions, such as theft or fighting, can bring out strong emotions. You want to do your best to present your complaint rationally and objectively and ensure that the disciplinary action is appropriate for the problem.

Document all disciplinary actions by recording:

- the date and time of the incident
- the date of the warning
- an accurate and objective description of the incident or problem behavior
- any mitigating factors
- results of any investigation that was required
- notations of the warning given
- future consequences
- summary of the employee's reaction and comments made at the disciplinary meeting itself

You may want to use a document like the Formal Warning Form on page 166. If you are giving this warning (as opposed to an undocumented verbal warning), write a description of the incident. "On May 12, you were seen taking a bag of pet food out to your car at the end of your shift. There is no record that you have paid for that bag of food." "On August 8, 10, and 17, you were ten to fifteen minutes late for your shift." "On Thursday, October 8, you were seen arguing with our client, Mrs. Jones. Mrs. Jones was unhappy that her bill was higher than she anticipated. As you discussed the bill with her, you and Mrs. Jones lost your temper. You were heard telling Mrs. Jones that if she didn't like our fees, she should leave and never come back."

Then, allow the employee to respond. This part of the form was intentionally kept simple. You do not want to argue the problem with a defensive employee. If you are sure enough of your facts to warrant disciplinary action, your employee should not have any room for debate. Your employee can mark whether or not she agrees with your description of the event. If there is a discrepancy, or if she feels that there is a material mitigating circumstance, she can write a response on the disciplinary form.

After you have presented the reprimand, give the employee an opportunity to present her position. Consider any mitigating factors. Take immediate action; provide additional training or counseling, or initiate disciplinary action. Before you take action, you might have another manager or veterinarian-owner review your disciplinary plan to ensure consistency and fair treatment.

Finish with the disciplinary action. Always advise the employee of the consequences if the problem behavior is not corrected. The consequence may be another warning, but it is often dismissal. Consider these questions:

- Are you simply putting the employee on notice that this behavior will not be tolerated?
- If you are giving a warning, what will happen the next time there is a similar incident?

- Is the infraction significant enough to warrant probation? An employee placed on probation is being told that she will not have a job at the end of the probationary period unless certain conditions are met. In this case, you need to identify the specific changes or improvements in performance that your employee needs to make to keep her job.
- How long are you going to give her to prove herself to you? Give your employee adequate time to show improvement. Typically, unless the problem involves health or safety issues, thirty to sixty days are given to resolve the problem. If the employee needs to stop cursing or being discourteous to clients, the behavior must stop immediately. She should be informed that another infraction shall result in dismissal. If the problem is poor performance, a retraining period may be appropriate before you expect improvement.

Once you define the problem and determine an appropriate resolution, as well as a workable time frame in which to resolve the problem, make sure that you monitor your employee for compliance.

By giving an employee a formal warning, you let her know how seriously you consider her performance and actions. This will give her a "heads up" that she must immediately modify her behavior or risk the stated consequences. A formal warning also gives you an opportunity to create a paper trail in case you need to justify an employee's termination.

BARE ESSENTIAL

When a warning is issued, advise the employee that the warning is now part of her employment record. You must be sure that you are willing to follow through and enforce stated consequences. Be sure that you are treating all employees equally.

You may be asked to support your decision to terminate an employee. You will want to be able to prove that the employee received notice of the reason for the warning or disciplinary action and counseling to correct her behavior. Another way to ensure that your action is appropriate is to have a higher authority (the owner

DISCIPLINARY ACTION AND LEGAL ISSUES

or practice manager, for example) approve any action that will result in termination and check that the action is consistent with prior similar incidents.

Table 10-1 lists recommended procedures to ensure good communications within your practice and to provide greater protection against lawsuits.

**TABLE 10-1
RECOMMENDED COMMUNICATION PROCEDURES**

These procedures are recommended to ensure good communications within your practice and to provide greater protection against lawsuits.

- Review all job descriptions and performance standards yearly.
- Ensure that your employees have the training, equipment, and time to do their job.
- Perform appraisals on an established schedule.
- Ensure that all reviewers and supervisors are familiar with the job duties and actual performance of employees whom they are rating.
- Provide annual training for all reviewers and supervisors on evaluating performance.
- Provide independent evaluation of reviews to look for retaliation, personal attacks, and discrimination.
- Require supervisors to identify and explain any dramatic decrease in the performance of their employee(s) and what actions they have taken to rectify the situation.
- Ensure that supervisors understand what defamatory statements are and the importance of avoiding their use.
- Establish a goal-setting system for all employees.
- Establish an appeals process for grievances after a review or disciplinary action.
- Have employees sign their appraisals to prove they received the information.

APPEALS AND ARBITRATION

One policy you should strongly consider implementing is an appeals process. It may benefit your hospital to have a procedure in place so that employees can complain about a perceived disparate or unjust assessment rather than pursue a civil remedy for their complaint. Courts are also more likely to dismiss the claims of an employee who has not taken advantage of an in-house grievance process.

In a midsize or large practice, there is often a practice manager, an owner, or a supervisor not directly involved in the review who can be designated to hear an employee's appeal. A set communication protocol and chain of command could be built for this process. This same grievance procedure could be used to handle grievances related to disciplinary action.

In a small practice, it may be difficult to establish an independent complaint system. Sometimes, there is only one person—the veterinarian-owner—who is the evaluator, the disciplinarian, and the decision-maker. It would be difficult for the owner, then, to also act as the complaint mediator. In this case, the practice might choose to use an outside mediator to resolve significant employee grievances.

Fortune 1000 companies are, according to a Cornell/Price WaterhouseCoopers Prevention and Early Resolution of Conflict (PERC) Alternative Dispute Resolution (ADR) survey, increasingly using outside mediators and arbitrators to resolve employment disputes. Mediation has been used by 79 percent of Fortune 1000 companies in the last three years, and 62 percent have used the services of an arbitrator, specifically for employment disputes. This may be a reasonable option for veterinary hospitals as well. Although it is an uncommon need, if you have a difficult situation with an employee that cannot be resolved internally, then a mediator or arbitrator may be the way to go. Either can be hired for individual cases and likely save you the cost and exposure of a lawsuit. If you would like to take advantage of this type of service, have new employees sign a standard written agreement stating that disputes will be resolved through the use of a mediator or arbitrator. To search for an arbitrator in your area, start by contacting the American Arbitration Association, Corporate Headquarters, 335 Madison Avenue, Floor 10, New York, NY 10017-4605, 212-716-5800.

DISCIPLINARY ACTION AND LEGAL ISSUES

DISMISSAL

Terminating an employee is a difficult and unpleasant task. However, termination is still a better option than retaining a substandard or undesirable employee. Any employee who has not responded to your call for job-appropriate performance, who continues to violate rules despite progressive warnings, or whose conduct causes imminent danger should be terminated. Here is a list of typical circumstances that warrant dismissal:

1. A new employee who is still in her trial period and does not meet the standards of the job.
2. The poorly performing employee who, in spite of prior warnings, has not satisfactorily improved her performance.
3. The employee who continues to violate policy despite progressive warnings.
4. The employee who makes such a serious mistake it warrants immediate dismissal. Such actions include theft, physical violence, and drug or alcohol abuse.

Managers often think they must give an employee three warnings before firing her. This is not the case. Having said that, if you have a progressive-discipline policy, you will be expected to follow that policy. That is why people mistakenly believe termination must follow certain steps. Gross or mounting misconduct can and should bypass progressive discipline. For example, an employee who uses abusive language, leaves early, and has another employee punch a time card for her may be terminated without your having to go through each step of progressive discipline for each transgression.

PRACTICAL CONSIDERATIONS

There are a number of issues to consider when you dismiss an employee. Some of the concerns are practical, and some are legal.

From a practical standpoint, your employee needs information when she is dismissed. First and foremost is a notice of separation and the true reason for the dismissal. If the dismissal is performance related, your review forms should back you up by proving that the employee was aware of and given the chance to correct substandard performance as well as a defined time frame in which to do it. As with the review itself, in any conflicted matter, objective examples will help your case. Instead of saying that your employee is being fired for a poor attitude, you can list specific examples of her unwillingness to assist customers or refusal to perform certain job tasks. When giving the reason for the dismissal, keep your answer concise. Do not get into a long discussion or argument with the employee about the reason for termination.

Years ago, I managed a nonprofit organization that served disabled adults. The director was a social worker. We had a substandard employee who was endangering the safety of some of the disabled adults we served. Despite having received training and two warnings, his job performance did not improve. The director and I decided it best to meet with him together for his termination. I advised him that I was terminating his employment and detailed the reason why. He wanted to argue and defend himself so that he would not lose this job. If the conversation had ended there, this episode would have been over. However, the social worker in the director took over. She was discussing his problems with him and trying to help. I could tell that she was getting dangerously close to letting him keep his job. I had to get the situation back on track quickly, terminate him, and end the meeting or risk the safety of the people we represented. *Once you have made a good decision to terminate someone, do not be swayed.*

Your employee also needs to know about continued benefits coverage, including health care (COBRA), vacation benefits, and unemployment-insurance benefits. It will certainly help the process if you are prepared with all of this information. It is also prudent to prepare a final paycheck, including any vacation, sick leave, or severance pay. Severance pay in lieu of notice is often given, not because the law requires it, but because it seems the decent thing to do. Be sure that any company property is returned before the employee leaves. If you believe that an employee's termination may go poorly, it would be wise to have a witness present. Whether or not you have a witness, you will also want to make notes of the meeting and place them in the employee's file.

Practically speaking, your employee is less likely to file a claim against you if she believes you have treated her decently. This means a fair decision based on company policy or progressive discipline and notification. It also means conducting the dismissal meeting privately and at an appropriate time of day.

When it comes to the law and employment issues, there are often gray areas. Many decisions are made on a case-by-case basis, resulting in interpretations you may not anticipate. This is precisely why a legal expert is a necessary resource for your practice.

Terminating the Employee

When an employee's work behavior justifies immediate termination, as in the case of violence or theft, or when substandard performance has been well documented, or progressive disciplinary action has been taken, go ahead and terminate the employee. Before doing so, doublecheck:

- that your actions are not discriminatory against a protected class of worker,
- that you have documented the situation, and
- that you are treating this employee in the same manner as you have treated other employees.

If you still end up in a lawsuit, answering to a wrongful-discharge claim, it will not be because you have acted improperly, and your records should justify your action. Always keep in mind that when you terminate an employee, you may end up in court no matter how well you have followed your policies and procedures and the law. However, if you have complied with the above recommendations, you are likely to win the lawsuit.

SUMMARY

Disciplinary action is appropriate for outrageous or illegal behavior, as well as for documented substandard performance. As long as the situation does not warrant immediate termination, a progressive disciplinary procedure is typically followed. The actions progress from a documented oral warning to a first written warning to a final warning before the employee is terminated.

Well-constructed performance reviews are critical to substantiating discharge based on poor performance. Established procedures and policies, as well as the use of a mediator or arbitrator, can help limit your potential for a lawsuit and the loss of a termination-related lawsuit.

In veterinary practice, employees are either under contract or are at-will. Contractual employees must be terminated according to the letter of the contract agreement. At-will employees may be terminated for any reason at any time as long as the termination is not based on discrimination against disability, age, sex, religion, national origin, race, or color, and it is not retaliatory. In terminating at-will employment, you must also avoid violating the exceptions of breach of implied contract, breach of implied covenant of good faith and fair dealing, and violation of public policy.

APPENDIX 1

Sample Employee Handbook Section on Employee Appraisals

ABC Hospital is committed to providing regular performance evaluations for every employee. Each employee will participate in an annual review with the manager and must provide any information requested for the evaluation. The review will be based on responsibilities outlined in each employee's job description and/or those responsibilities tacitly understood based on training and conversations regarding responsibilities.

The review is a written evaluation of work performance and achievements. It is also a record of performance problems. At the review, the employee and manager will establish performance objectives.

APPENDIX 2

SOFTWARE PROGRAMS

A number of software programs are available to assist you in conducting your employee evaluations. The programs range from the Employee Appraiser by Austin Hayne for about $100 to Visual 360, a world-review system by MindSolve Technologies for $25,000. As you might expect, the software for the more complex world review tends to be more expensive than the software for a traditional review. Many of the world- or 360-degree review software programs are cost-prohibitive for the average veterinary practice. However, if you maintain a paperless practice or have a large number of employees, the software may be worth the investment for you. You can purchase a highly rated world review software program for $2,000. You also have the option of purchasing a web-based system.

Employee-appraisal software offers review templates that can often be customized to your needs. The programs tabulate the results and may help set goals based on the data. They often include examples or suggested phrases to assist you with your process. Some programs include articles or training in the review process itself, as well as guidance on other personnel issues.

Listed on the next page is contact information for some of the programs that are currently available.

Performance Now!
Knowledge Point
1129 Industrial Ave
Petaluma, CA 94952-1141
800-727-1133 / 707-762-0333
www.knowledgepoint.com
Price: $119.00
Special Features: Other HR modules available

Employee Appraiser
Success Factors, Inc.
2929 Campus Drive, Suite 400
San Mateo, CA 94403
800-809-9920 / 650-475-5800

20/20 Insight Gold
Performance Support Systems
11835 Canon Blvd.
Suite C-101
Newport News, VA 23606
800-488-6463 / 757-873-3700
www.2020insight.net
Price: $3,500-$6,175 but single-usage license also available starting at $60/use/subject
Also available through distributors

CompStar Appraiser Plus 360
Questar Info Comm
180 East 100 South
Salt Lake City, UT 84111
888-266-7782
www.compstarhrsolutions.com
Price: $50/employee for businesses with less than 60 employees
Special Features: Has a veterinary line of software, web-based

Corporate Pulse and Pulse Tools
Praxis/Vitality Alliance
55 N. University Ave. Suite 225
Provo, Utah 84601
www.vitalityalliance.com
801-373-2233
Price: $3,500

APPENDIX 3

FORMS

Note: This form is also available on the disk that accompanies this book. Please feel free to modify it for your needs.

WORLD EVALUATION FORM

Employee name _____

Evaluation period _____

Due date _____

Please rate this employee in each performance area on a scale of one to ten using the following guidelines. You must make specific comments for your reason for any rating of five or less. It is extremely helpful if you can give examples of how this employee fails or succeeds in each performance area. Provide specific suggestions for improvement.

1 Very poor performance; employee needs a great deal of improvement in this area
3 Needs improvement in this area
5 Average; adequate ability or performance in this area
7 Very good; better than average in this area
10 Could not improve any further in this area

Client Relations

Has good phone manner and skills	1	2	3	4	5	6	7	8	9	10
Deals with clients quickly and efficiently	1	2	3	4	5	6	7	8	9	10
Is pleasant to clients	1	2	3	4	5	6	7	8	9	10

Knowledge Base

Has knowledge of products sold and dispensed	1	2	3	4	5	6	7	8	9	10
Has knowledge of basic medical problems and policies and procedures	1	2	3	4	5	6	7	8	9	10
Has knowledge of technical procedures	1	2	3	4	5	6	7	8	9	10
Has computer knowledge	1	2	3	4	5	6	7	8	9	10
Wants to learn	1	2	3	4	5	6	7	8	9	10
Is able to learn	1	2	3	4	5	6	7	8	9	10

WORLD EVALUATION FORM (cont'd)

Team Skills

Has a good attitude		1 2 3 4 5 6 7 8 9 10
Is cooperative		1 2 3 4 5 6 7 8 9 10
Does not avoid any aspect of job		1 2 3 4 5 6 7 8 9 10

General Skills

Communicates effectively		1 2 3 4 5 6 7 8 9 10
Has effective animal handling skills		1 2 3 4 5 6 7 8 9 10
Is efficient, productive, accurate		1 2 3 4 5 6 7 8 9 10
Is punctual and dependable		1 2 3 4 5 6 7 8 9 10
Maintains composure		1 2 3 4 5 6 7 8 9 10
Responds well to feedback/comments		1 2 3 4 5 6 7 8 9 10
Is adaptable		1 2 3 4 5 6 7 8 9 10
Takes initiative		1 2 3 4 5 6 7 8 9 10
Exercises good judgment		1 2 3 4 5 6 7 8 9 10
Handles multiple tasks concurrently		1 2 3 4 5 6 7 8 9 10
Has a presentable, professional appearance		1 2 3 4 5 6 7 8 9 10
Maintains a clean working environment		1 2 3 4 5 6 7 8 9 10
Follows instructions well		1 2 3 4 5 6 7 8 9 10

Comments: (continue on back)

WORLD EVALUATION FORM (cont'd)

Goals from last period **Met** **Unmet**

1.

2.

3.

4.

5.

Summary

Attendance satisfactory   Yes_____   No_____

Overall evaluation of employee's performance based on all scores (scale of 1 – 10) _____

Employee's strengths:

Employee's weaknesses:

Development goals: **To be achieved by:**

Areas that need to be addressed or improved for employee to continue in current position:

Signature of employee indicates receipt of appraisal. It does not necessarily indicate agreement.

Employee signature _____ Date _____

Employer signature _____ Date _____

Note: A blank sample of this form is available on the disk that accompanies this book.

COMPLETED WORLD EVALUATION FORM

Employee name _____Kristen Moore_____

Evaluation period_____1/1/XX-12/31/XX_____

Due date _____1/15/XX_____

Please rate this employee in each performance area on a scale of one to ten using the following guidelines. You must make specific comments for any rating of five or less. It is extremely helpful if you can give examples of how this employee fails or succeeds in each performance area. Provide specific suggestions for improvement.

1 Very poor performance; employee needs a great deal of improvement in this area
3 Needs improvement in this area
5 Average; adequate ability or performance in this area
7 Very good; better than average in this area
10 Could not improve any further in this area

Client Relations

Has good phone manner and skills	6.8
Deals with clients quickly and efficiently	8.1
Is pleasant to clients	8.3
Average for Client Relations:	**7.7**

Knowledge Base

Has knowledge of products sold and dispensed	8.4
Has knowledge of basic medical medical problems and policies and procedures	6.9
Has knowledge of technical procedures	3.5
Has computer knowledge	7.3
Wants to learn	5.0
Is able to learn	4.9
Average for Knowledge Base:	**6.0**

COMPLETED WORLD EVALUATION FORM (cont'd)

Team Skills

Has a good attitude	6.8
Is cooperative	7.4
Does not avoid any aspect of job	7.7
Average for Team Skills:	**7.3**

General Skills

Communicates effectively	8.0
Has effective animal handling skills	3.2
Is efficient, productive, accurate	8.4
Is punctual and dependable	10.0
Maintains composure	7.1
Responds well to feedback/comments	4.8
Is adaptable	6.9
Takes initiative	7.2
Exercises good judgment	5.1
Handles multiple tasks concurrently	7.8
Has a presentable, professional appearance	9.3
Maintains a clean working environment	8.4
Follows instructions well	7.4
Average for General Skills:	**7.2**

COMPLETED WORLD EVALUATION FORM (cont'd)

Comments:
Kristen has worked only as a receptionist and has no training in technical areas, including restraint. Kristen is great at handling difficult clients—she even keeps Melinda Johnson happy. She is very professional; always on time and looking good. She always keeps an extra smock handy to be sure she looks presentable.

In July, when we lost our air-conditioning, Kristen took charge and called the repairman. She made sure all the clients and pets in the waiting and exam rooms had water and were comfortable.

I have noticed that Kristen doesn't always attend our optional continuing-education meetings. I don't think she's interested in the technical side at all. It would help if she would at least be able to do a good job of holding animals for shots and blood draws.

Points for discussion with supervisor:
- Bravos for initiative, client relations, professionalism
- Would value improvement in general knowledge/technical skills and restraint (although not critical for success in her position)

Goals from last period	Met	Unmet
1. Improve animal-handling skills to be able to restrain dogs and cats for routine procedures		X
2. Attend seminar on phone techniques	X	

Summary
Attendance satisfactory   Yes __X__   No_____

Overall evaluation of employee's performance based on all scores (scale of 1 – 10) __7.0__

Employee's strengths:
Professionalism (appearance, dependability, job well done)
Client interaction

Employee's weaknesses:
Technical skills
Animal restraint

Development goals:	To be achieved by:
1. Improve animal restraint—will work with technician 30 minutes per week	3/31/20XX
2. Learn desktop publishing software program and produce hospital newsletter	6/30/20XX

Areas that need to be addressed or improved for employee to continue in current position: None

COMPLETED WORLD EVALUATION FORM

Employee name _____ Marcy Brown _____

Evaluation period _____ 3/15/XX-3/15/XX _____

Due date _____ 3/20/XX _____

Please rate this employee in each performance area on a scale of one to ten using the following guidelines. You must make specific comments for any rating of five or less. It is extremely helpful if you can give examples of how this employee fails or succeeds in each performance area. Provide specific suggestions for improvement.

1. Very poor performance; employee needs a great deal of improvement in this area
3. Needs improvement in this area
5. Average; adequate ability or performance in this area
7. Very good; better than average in this area
10. Could not improve any further in this area

Client Relations

Has good phone manner and skills	3.1
Deals with clients quickly and efficiently	3.0
Is pleasant to clients	2.9
Average Client Relations:	**3.0**

Knowledge Base

Has knowledge of products sold and dispensed	4.7
Has knowledge of basic medical problems, and policies and procedures	5.2
Has knowledge of technical procedures	2.2
Has computer knowledge	5.0
Wants to learn	4.8
Is able to learn	5.1
Average Knowledge Base:	**4.5**

COMPLETED WORLD EVALUATION FORM (cont'd)

Team Skills

Has a good attitude	2.9
Is cooperative	3.1
Does not avoid any aspect of job	5.0
Average Team Skills:	**3.7**

General Skills

Communicates effectively	3.2
Has effective animal handling skills	5.1
Is efficient, productive, accurate	3.8
Is punctual and dependable	7.6
Maintains composure	5.0
Responds well to feedback/comments	2.8
Is adaptable	4.2
Takes initiative	4.9
Exercises good judgment	5.5
Handles multiple tasks concurrently	4.9
Has a presentable, professional appearance	7.2
Maintains a clean working environment	6.1
Follows instructions well	4.7
Average General Skills:	**5.0**

Comments:
Marcy seems to think that she is pleasant to clients, but she really isn't. She can be very blunt and unsympathetic. When callers ask for a price estimate, she has been heard saying that they shouldn't be asking, that they should just have the procedure done. Last week, Mrs. Johnson asked for help taking a bag of dog food out and Marcy wouldn't help her.

COMPLETED WORLD EVALUATION FORM (cont'd)

Comments (cont'd):

Marcy doesn't smile when she is talking on the phone and may come across badly. She says "uh" and "you know" a lot. She doesn't always acknowledge clients when they walk in. The worst, though, was when she was gossiping about a client and a client in the waiting room overheard her.

Marcy doesn't have any technical skills to speak of and hasn't been willing to learn to help with emergencies. She just wants to stick with receptionist duties. Because she hasn't been willing to help deal with emergencies, she's not really part of the team. Marcy has also had difficulty picking up the pace when people are waiting.

Points for discussion with supervisor:
- Employed six months as receptionist; should be showing more client skills
- Concentrate discussion on specific examples and solutions in this area.

Goals from last period	**Met**	**Unmet**
1. Learn more about products we carry	X	
2. Run end-of-month reports	X	

Summary

Attendance satisfactory   Yes _____   No __X__

Overall evaluation of employee's performance based on all scores (scale of 1 – 10) __4.5__

Employee's strengths:
Presentability
Cleanliness

Employee's weaknesses:
Client interaction
Technical knowledge
Communication skills

Development goals:	**To be achieved by:**
More effective communication	6/15/XX
More effective client interaction	6/15/XX
Weekly meetings with supervisor	6/15/XX
Attend communication seminar	6/15/XX
Daily mentoring by selected receptionist	6/15/XX

Areas that need to be addressed or improved for employee to continue in current position:
Cooperation
Client-relation skills

Note: This form is also available on the disk that accompanies this book. Please feel free to modify it for your needs.

TRADITIONAL EVALUATION FORM

Employee Name _____

Review period _____

Position _____

Due date _____

	Does not meet requirements	Inconsistently meets requirements	Consistently meets requirements	Exceeds job requirements	Far exceeds job requirements
1. Attendance/punctuality	___	___	___	___	___
2. Client interaction	___	___	___	___	___
3. Communication skills	___	___	___	___	___
4. Technical skills	___	___	___	___	___
5. Knowledge base	___	___	___	___	___
6. Productivity	___	___	___	___	___
7. Attitude	___	___	___	___	___
8. Efficiency and accuracy	___	___	___	___	___
9. Professional appearance	___	___	___	___	___
10. Organization/cleanliness	___	___	___	___	___
11. Cooperation	___	___	___	___	___
12. Initiative	___	___	___	___	___
13. Adaptability	___	___	___	___	___
Overall performance	___	___	___	___	___

TRADITIONAL EVALUATION FORM (cont'd)

Goals met from last period:

Goals unmet from last period:

Employee's strengths:

Specific examples of major achievement:

Development needs:

Future goals/development plan

Goal:_____To be achieved by:

Employee comments:

Signature of employee indicates receipt of appraisal. It does not necessarily indicate agreement.

Employee signature _____ Date _____

Employer signature _____ Date _____

COMPLETED TRADITIONAL EVALUATION FORM

Employee Name ____Mark Henault_____

Review period ____1/1/XX-6/30/XX_____

Position ____Technician_____

Due date ____7/15/XX____

	Does not meet requirements	Inconsistently meets requirements	Consistently meets requirements	Exceeds job requirements	Far exceeds job requirements
1. Attendance/punctuality			X		
2. Client interaction		X			
3. Communication skills		X			
4. Technical skills			X		
5. Knowledge base				X	
6. Productivity			X		
7. Attitude			X		
8. Efficiency and accuracy			X		
9. Professional appearance		X			
10. Organization/cleanliness			X		
11. Cooperation			X		
12. Initiative			X		
13. Adaptability			X		
Overall performance			**X**		

COMPLETED TRADITIONAL EVALUATION FORM (cont'd)

Goals met from last period:
Learned to use new dental equipment
Attended CE seminar

Goals unmet from last period:
None

Employee's strengths:
Knowledge base
Ability to comfort patients
Technical skills

Specific examples of major achievement:
Worked with manufacturer of new dental equipment to set it up and train the staff.

Development needs:
Client interaction: Sometimes seems uncomfortable and awkward with clients, resulting in poor information exchange.

Future goals/development plan

Goal:_____ To be achieved by:
Improve client communication: 9/30/XX
    Shadow receptionist
    Cross-train at front desk
    Watch AAHA videotape on client
       communication

Employee comments:

Signature of employee indicates receipt of appraisal. It does not necessarily indicate agreement.

Employee signature _____ Date _____

Employer signature _____ Date _____

Note: This form is also available on the disk that accompanies this book. Please feel free to modify it for your needs.

FORMAL COMMENDATION

Name _____

Date _____

Date of event _____

Description of event:

Specific reason for commendation:

Signature of manager _____

Signature of employee _____

COMPLETED FORMAL COMMENDATION

Name   Nancy Ulster

Date   9/7/XX

Date of event   9/7/XX

Description of event:

Samantha Richards called this morning to get an appointment to bring her dog in because he was unable to walk. Because Samantha is eight months pregnant and Charlie (her dog) weighs 100 pounds, she could not get him in the car by herself. Nancy went to Samantha's house during her lunch hour and put Charlie in the car so that he could be brought to the hospital to be evaluated.

Specific reason for commendation:

Terrific client service—above and beyond the call of duty

Signature of manager _____

Signature of employee _____

Note: This form is also available on the disk that accompanies this book. Please feel free to modify it for your needs.

FORMAL WARNING

Employee name _____

Date of warning _____

Date of incident _____

Time _____

Description of incident:

Employee statement:

I agree _____ disagree _____ with the above statement and/or description. If there is disagreement, description of event from employee viewpoint:

Action: Warning _____

                Probation _____

                Suspension _____

Should a similar incident occur, the employee will be
_____
_____

Signature of employee _____ Date _____

Signature of employer _____ Date _____

COMPLETED FORMAL WARNING

Employee name _____Sharon Lehman_____

Date of warning ___4/12/XX_____

Date of incident _____4/11/XX_____

Time _____9:15 A.M._____

Description of incident:

Sharon was scheduled to start her shift at 8:45 A.M. She arrived and clocked in at 9:15 A.M.

Employee statement:

I agree _____ disagree _____ with the above statement and/or description. If there is disagreement, description of event from employee viewpoint:

Action: Warning ___X_____

Probation _____

Suspension _____

Should a similar incident occur, the employee will be

_____put on probation_____

Signature of employee _____ Date _____

Signature of employer _____ Date _____

REFERENCES

Christopher J. Allen, DVM, JD, "Lawsuits for Wrongful Discharge: What's the Prognosis for Your Practice?" DVM *Newsmagazine*, May 1995.

Anthony A. Atkinson et al., "A Stakeholder Approach to Strategic Performance Measurement." *Sloan Management Review*, Spring 1995, Vol. 38, No. 3.

Beth Caldwell, "What To Do When Employees Use Drugs." VPM *Magazine*, Winter 1988-89.

Joanne W. Clevenger, "Good Performance Reviews Can Raise Morale and Improve Client Relations." *Journal of the American Veterinary Medical Association*, Vol. 206, No. 2 (January 15, 1995).

Mark R. Edwards and Ann J. Ewen, 360° *Feedback*. New York: Amacom, 1996.

Sheldon I. London, *How To Comply with Federal Employee Laws*. Rochester, N.Y.: VIZIA, 2000.

P.M. Perry, "Flawed Evaluations Could Cost You Plenty." *Veterinary Economics*, July 1994, pp. 58-63.

Cameron D. Reynolds and Morgan O. Reynolds, "State Court Restrictions on the Employment-at-Will Doctrine." *The Cato Review of Business and Government*, 2000.

Jack Stack, "The Curse of the Annual Performance Review," *Inc. Magazine*, March 1997.

David A. Waldman and Leanne E. Atwater, *The Power of 360° Feedback*. Houston, Tex.: Gulf Publishing Company, 1998.

Elizabeth Welborn, "Sticky Situations: How to Approach A Colleague." TRENDS *Magazine*, August/September 1996.

Age Discrimination in Employment Act. 29 U.S.C. 621–634.

Americans with Disabilities Act of 1990. 42 U.S.C. 12101.

Civil Rights Act of 1964. 42 U.S.C. Chapter 21.

Ebbing *v.* Masco, Mich., No. 60907, 1980.

Employment Discrimination: An Overview. Legal Information Institute, 2000.

Employment Law Resource Center, Alexander Hamilton Institute, Ramsey, N.J., 1999.

Facts About Pregnancy Discrimination, U.S. Equal Employment and Opportunity Commission, 2000.

Fortune *v.* National Cash Register, 364 N.E. 2d 1251, 1977.

Karpel *v.* Inova Health Systems, 4th Cir., WL 25699, 1998.

Monge *v.* Beebe Rubber Company, 316 A. 2d 549, N.H., 1974.

Occupational Safety and Health Act of 1970.

Palmatee *v.* International Harvester, Ill., No. 53780, 1981.

Performance Appraisals. Society for Human Resource Management, 1998.

Personnel Legal Alerts. Ramsey, N.J.: Alexander Hamilton Institute, 1999.

Petermann *v.* Teamsters Local 396, Cal. Ct. App., 1959.

Safeway Stores *v.* Retail Clerks, Cal., 1953.

"Top Tips for Avoiding Performance Appraisal Mistakes," *Manager's Legal Bulletin*. Ramsey, N.J.: Alexander Hamilton Institute, 1995.

Toussaint *v.* Blue Cross and Blue Shield of Michigan, Mich., No. 60917, 1980.

Weiner *v.* McGraw-Hill, Inc., New York, New York, No. 485, 1982.

Employee handbooks and appraisal forms from selected businesses and universities.

INDEX

A

Absenteeism, 132
Absolutes, avoiding, 106
Abuse, substance, 132, 133, 141
Accuracy, in work, 57-59, 81
Achievements, of employees, 22, 67
Adaptability, as criterion for evaluation, 65, 82
Advancement, opportunities for, 113
Age Discrimination in Employment Act, 127
All positions in a veterinary practice
    Accuracy, as criterion for evaluation, 58
    Attitude, as criterion for evaluation, 57
    Cleanliness of employees, 60-61
    Cooperation, as criterion for evaluation, 63
    Efficiency, as criterion for evaluation, 58
    Professional appearance, as criterion for evaluation, 59-60
    Skills to emphasize, 37
American Arbitration Association, 140
Americans with Disabilities Act of 1990, 127
Anger, of employee, 117
Animal handling skills, 37, 80
Anonymity of reviewers, in world review, 31, 36, 44, 89
Anxiety, of employee, 117
Appeals, 139-140
Appraisal, performance. *See also* Reviews, employee
    As a legal document, 124-125
Arbitration, 139-140
Arguing, 20
    With employee during review meeting, 107-108
Attendance, 48-49, 92
Attitude, 12, 37, 57

B

Bare Essential icons, 11, 13, 16, 17, 19, 33, 42, 72, 97, 103, 106, 112, 113, 123, 132, 135, 138, 143
    Explanation of, 2
Barriers, to effective communication, 113-118
Being specific, importance of, 13, 42, 67, 68
    During the review meeting, 106
    In goal setting, 97
    In world reviews, 72
Belittling, of other staff members, 29
Benchmarks, industry, 76
Benefits
    After dismissal, 142
    Of the review, 3-10

Best Results. *See* For Best Results
Bias, in a review, 24, 25, 39, 41. *See also* Errors, potential
    Self-bias, 41
Blaming others, for errors, 20
Blandness, as a communication barrier, 115
Body piercing, 60
Bonding, of employee to practice, 6
Bonuses, 119
    Year-end, 11
Booklet, employee, 2
Breach of an implied contract, 128-129
Breach of implied covenant of good faith and fair dealing, 129-130
Breaches, in policy, 21
Business plan, changes in, 19

C
Central tendency, 41. *See also* Errors, potential
Choosing the right kind of review, 23-29
Civil Rights Act of 1964, 127
"Clam" behaviors of employee during the review, 118
Cleanliness, 37, 60-61
Client
    Interaction, 37, 49-50, 67, 77-78
    Relations, as performance criteria, 77
    Satisfaction, tracking, 41
Clients
    As evaluators in the world review, 26, 32
    Bonding with, 18
Coaching situations, 23, 26
COBRA, 142
Collusion, among employees, 44
Commendation, formal, 22, 164, 165
Commitment, of employee to the practice, 4, 5-6
Communication
    And the world review, 26
    Barriers to effective, 113-118.
Communication, open, 113
    As a means to enhance performance, 5, 12
Communication, poor, as a reason for job dissatisfaction, 4
Communication skills, 37, 50-51
Comparisons, between employees, 109-110
    Resentment caused by, 110
Compliments, 21
CompStar Appraiser Plus 360, 148
Computer records, use of, 34-35
Consequences, of poor performance, 16, 21

Consistency, in conducting reviews, 11
Contrast error, 42. *See also* Errors, potential
Conversation, example of during review meeting, 111-112
Cooperation, among staff, 62-63
Corporate Pulse and Pulse Tools, 148
Cost-of-living adjustments, 118-119
Criteria
    Objective, 39, 40, 42
    Performance, 48-65. *See also* Performance criteria
    Subjective, 39, 40
Criticism, of employee, 105
Crying, by employee during review, 117
Culture, of the practice, 114
Cursing, 109, 141

D
Damages, economic, 131
Damage, to company property, 132
Data, gathering of, 24
    And the world review, 26
    Frequency, 24
    Objective, 40, 92, 106, 136
    Subjective, 40, 92
Day one, for new employees, 12-13
    Important goals for employer, 12-13
Demoralization, of staff, 17
Developmental opportunities, 69
Disagreements, resolution of, 107
Discharge. *See also* Dismissal, Termination
    Substantiation for, 88
    Wrongful, 129, 134
Disciplinary action, 101, 131-144
    Importance of documenting, 136-137
    Progressive, 133-134
    Reasons to take, 132-133
    Verbal warnings, 133, 134-135
    Written warnings, 133, 135-139
Discourtesy, 132
Discrepant responder, 44, 89
Discrimination, 124
Dishonesty, 132
Dismissal, 141-144. *See also* Discharge, Termination
    Circumstances that warrant, 141
    Practical considerations regarding, 141-143
    Terminating the employee, 142-144

Distress, emotional, 131
Doctors. *See* Veterinarians
Documenting
    Of breaches in policy, 21
    Of disciplinary action, 136-137
    Of work performance, 5
Does not avoid any aspect of job, as criterion for evaluation, 75, 80
Does not meet requirements, as a rating, 48
Dress code, violation of, 132
Drugs, selling, 132-133

E
Ebling *v.* Masco Corp., 129
Efficiency, in work, 57-59, 81
Emergencies, ability to handle, 63
Emotional responses, to the review, 116-118
    The clam, 118
    The crier, 117
    The silent sufferer, 118
    The volcano, 117-118
Employee Appraiser, 148
Employee Handbook, 145
Employees
    Contract, 126-127
    Empowered, 26, 73
    Encouraging improvement of performance, 9
    Encouraging pursuit of mutual goals with, 6-10
    Established, 18-20
    Goals for newly hired, 14-15
    Improving performance of, 4-5
    New, 12-18
    Preparation for the review, 31-38
    Strengthening commitment of, 5-6
    Task-oriented, 115
    Who do not seem to care, 9-10
Employee's Guide to the Performance Appraisal, 48, 71
Employment-at-will, 126-131
    Breach of implied contract, 128-129
    Breach of implied covenant of good faith and fair dealing, 129-130
    Contract employees, 126-127
    Exceptions to employment-at-will doctrine, 127-128
    Protected classes, 127
    Violation of public policy, 130-131
Empowerment, of employees, 73
Environment, working, improvement of, 6
Equitable treatment, importance of, 12
Error of recency, 40. *See also* Errors, potential

Error of similarity, 42. *See also* Errors, potential
Error of stereotyping, 42-43. *See also* Errors, potential
Errors, potential
    Bias, 41
    Central tendency, 41
    Contrast, 42
    Elimination of in world review, 43-44
    Error of recency, 33, 40
    Error of similarity, 42
    Error of stereotyping, 42-43
    Halo effect, 40
    In conducting employee reviews, 19
    Leniency, 41-42
    One-experience effect, 43
    Strictness, 41-42
Evaluations
    Building useful evaluations, 36-38
    Disparities between employee and employer, 104
    Importance of honesty in, 29
    Of a performance appraisal, 120-121
    Putting into perspective, 104
Evaluators, and the world review, 26
Examples, of work performance
    Importance of giving examples, 67, 87
Exceeds job requirements, as a rating, 47
Experience Talking icons, 8, 9, 20, 44, 62, 73, 75, 88, 97, 104, 108, 114, 141, 142
    Explanation of, 2

F
Feedback, importance of, 4, 18, 19, 21, 22
Feedback system
    Faults of, 33
    To evaluators in a world review, 44
    With world review, 26
Felony conviction, 132
Fighting, 132, 136
Financial and Productivity Pulsepoints: A Comprehensive Survey and Analysis of Benchmark and Performance Data, 76
Financial management skills, 38
First days, on the job, 12-13
Focus, maintaining during review meeting, 108-109
Formality, importance of maintaining in a review, 101
For Best Results icons, 12, 19, 21, 26, 31, 33, 42, 44, 65, 67, 86, 87, 94, 99, 103, 105, 107, 109, 115, 118, 135, 142
    Explanation of, 2
Formal Comendation Form, 164
    Completed, 165

A PRACTICAL GUIDE TO PERFORMANCE APPRAISALS

Formal Warning Form, 137, 166
    Completed, 167
Forms
    Commendation, 164-165
    Designing your own, 36
    Standard, 36
    Traditional evaluation, 160-163
    Warning, 166-167
    World evaluation, 151-159
Friendship, and its relationship to respondents in a world review, 43

G

General skills, as performance criteria, 80-83
    Communicates effectively, 80
    Exercises good judgment, 82
    Follows instructions well, 83
    Handles multiple tasks concurrently, 83
    Has effective animal handling skills, 80
    Has presentable, professional appearance
    Is adaptable, 82
    Is efficient, productive, accurate, 81
    Is punctual and dependable, 81
    Maintains clean working environment, 83
    Maintains composure, 81
    Responds well to feedback/comments, 82
Goals, for the practice, 98
Goals, individual, 8, 35
    Being specific in, 98
    Evaluation of, 19, 66
    For new employees, 13, 14-15, 22
    Priority goals, 98
    Resetting, 16, 19
    Setting, 97-100, 111-113
    To correct deficiencies, 98
Goals, mutual, 4, 5, 6-10, 35, 113
    As a way to track employee progress, 7-8, 66
    Discussion of, 7-8
    Setting, 97-100, 101, 111-113
    Sharing with employees who do not care, 9-10
    To correct deficiencies, 98
Goals, personal, 99-100
    Accommodation of, 99
    Being specific in setting, 99
    Breaking down into manageable steps, 100
    Setting time frame for, 99-100
Goodwill *v.* Oklahoma Department of Corrections, 134

Gossiping, 20
Grievance process, in-house, 140
Groomers, skills to emphasize, 37

H
Halo effect, 40-41. *See also Errors*, potential
Harassment, sexual, 132
Headaches, of employee during review, 118
History, past, dwelling on, 109

I
Icons, explanation of, 2
Improvement, determining where employee needs, 68-70
Informal sit-downs, 16
Information gathering, 24, 33-35
    From computer and paper records, 34-35
    From employees, 33
Information tracking, 34
Initiative, 63-65, 69-70, 82, 110
Insubordination, 132
Integrity, lack of, 116
Intimidation, feelings of by employee, 114, 117
Investment, in goals of the practice, 112
Issues, personal, 110
    Preventing during review meeting, 106, 107

J
Job dissatisfaction, 4

K
Kennel assistants, 9-10, 43, 49, 69
    Accuracy evaluation, 58
    Efficiency evaluation, 58
    Goals for newly hired, 15
    Knowledge base for, 54
    Productivity in work, evaluation of, 56
    Skills to emphasize, 37
    Technical skills for, 51
Knowledge base, 37, 53-55
    As performance criterion, 78-79
    Computer knowledge, 79
    Is able to learn, 79
    Knowledge of basic medical problems and policies and procedures, 78
    Knowledge of products sold and dispensed, 78
    Knowledge of technical procedures, 78
    Wants to learn, 79

L

Language, abusive. *See* Cursing
Law, employment, 123-144
Leadership abilities, 38
Learning, continuous, commitment to, 73
Legal issues, 123-144
Leniency, 41-42. *See also* Errors, potential

M

Management by objectives, 23
Management system, open, 26
Managers, 23, 24, 50, 76
    Accounts receivable handling, 84
    Accuracy, as criterion for evaluation, 59
    Bookkeeping skills, 85
    Business, 32
    Efficiency, as criterion for evaluation, 59
    Financial skills, 86
    Forecasting skills, 85
    General managerial skills, 86
    Human resource skills, 85
    Initiative, as criterion for evaluation, 65
    Inventory management, 32, 84
    Knowledge base for, 55
    Leadership skills, as criteria for evaluation, 76
    Marketing skills, 85
    Office, 35
    Organizational skills needed for, 62
    Planning skills, 85
    Productivity in work, evaluation of, 57
    Reviews of, 38
    Skills to emphasize, 37
    Special evaluation of, 84-86
    Supervisory skills, as criteria for evaluation, 76
    Technical skills for, 53
Mediators, use of, 140
Medical abilities, 38
Meetings
    Formal, 33
    Informal, 13
Meets job requirements, as a rating, 47
Michigan Supreme Court, 128-129
Minoritie, and self-bias, 41
Minor points, belaboring, 109, 113
Misconduct, 141
    Off-duty, 132

Misdemeanor conviction, 132
Money, as a motivator, 9
Monge *v.* Beebe Rubber Company, 130
Month one, for new employees, 16-17
Month three, for new employees, 17-18
Moonlighting, at competitor's practice, 132
Multiple roles, in a veterinary practice, 73
Multirater review, 23, 25. *See also* World review

N
Nausea, by employee during the review, 118
Needs, of practice, for the future, 111
Neutral ground, as setting for review site, 102
Note taking
    During informal meeting, 16
    Throughout the year, 33, 40
    To assess progress, 43

O
Objectivity, 47, 55, 106
Occupational Safety and Health Act of 1970, 127
One-experience effect, 43. *See also* Errors, potential
Opportunities for further development, 68
Organizational skills, 37, 61-62
Organizer, extreme, 62

P
Palmatee *v.* International Harvester, 131
Paper trails, importance of creating, 138
Performance, acceptable, 5
Performance criteria, 48-65. *See also* individual entries for each criterion
    Adaptability, 65, 82
    Attendance/punctuality, 48-49
    Attitude, 12, 37, 57
    Cleanliness, 37, 60-61
    Client interaction, 49-50
    Communication skills, 50-51
    Cooperation, 62-63
    Initiative, 63-65, 69-70, 82, 110
    Knowledge base, 78-79
    Organization, 37, 61-62
    Productivity, 6, 37, 55-57, 81
    Professionall appearance, 37, 59-60, 83
    Technical skills, 37, 51-53
Performance, employee
    Fine-tuning, 19

How to improve, 4-5
    Improvement of in preparation for the review, 40 . *See also* Error of recency
    Overall, 65-70
Performance, ideal, 5
Performance Now!, 148
Performance, substandard, 17, 105-107
Personal calls, while at work, 21
Personal issues. *See* Issues, personal
Personality traits, how they affect the review, 115-116
Personnel management skills, 38
Petermann *v.* Teamsters Local 396, 130
Pets, bonding with, 18
Pharmacy manager, and organizational skills, 61
Phone manner and skills, 77
Pitfalls, potential, in conducting a review, 39-45
    Eliminating errors in world review, 43-44
    Errors, 39-43
Plans, for the practice, 6
Policies, written, 125-126
Practice
    Large, 140
    Midsize, 140
    Personality of, 23
    Philosophy of, 23
    Potential of, 18
    Small, 140
Praise, importance of, 4
Preparation, for reviews, 31-38
    Employee, 31-32
Probation, 138
Problems
    Identification, 5, 17
    Nipping in the bud, 13
    Personal problems of employee, 20, 107, 110
    Resolution of, 5, 108
    Serious, 20
Procedures
    Number of completed, 39
    Recommended to ensure good communication and to avoid lawsuits, 139
    Written, advantages of having, 125-126
Productivity, 6, 37, 55-57, 81
    Evaluation of, 34, 35
    Prediction of employee's, 34
Professional appearance, 37, 59-60, 83
Progress check, six-month, 12, 19-20
Protected classes, 127

Public policy, violation of, 130-131
Punctuality, 37, 48-49, 107

Q
Quality, in work, 56
Questions to ask, before filling out review form, 35

R
Radiographic duty, 34
Raises, merit, 119
    When employee attempts to negotiate, 120
Rating scales, 23, 72
    Numerical, 74-75
Ratings
    During the review meeting, 103-105
    Manipulation of, 43-44
    Variations in, 43
    When they are useful, 43
Recent history, errors regarding performance, 33
Receptionists, 34, 35, 43, 49, 67, 68-69, 111
    Accuracy, as criterion for evaluation, 58
    Efficiency, as criterion for evaluation, 58
    Goals for newly hired, 15
    Initiative, as criterion for evaluation, 64
    Knowledge base for, 53-54, 69
    Organizational skills needed for, 61
    Productivity in work, evaluation of, 56
    Scheduling appointments, 34
    Skills to emphasize, 37
    Technical skills for, 51
Recognition, importance of, 22
Record keeping
    Of everyday performance, 33
Remembering specific events, 40
Reports, running of in practice, 8
Reprimands, 16, 101, 166-167. *See also* Warnings
    Formal, 131, 166-167
Requirements, of job
    Does not meet, 48
    Exceeds, 48
    Meets, 47
Reviewers, of employees, 24
    And the traditional review, 160-163
    And the world review, 26, 151-159
Review forms, 33
Review meeting, 101-121

General tips for, 107-111
Goal setting during, 111-113
Length of time for, 102
Outlining purpose of and ground rules for, 102
Performance problems, discussing, 105-107
Preliminaries to, 101-103
Ratings during, 103-105
Summarization of, 113

Reviews, employee
Annual, 11
Benefits of, 3-10
Faults of, 33
Preparation for, 31-38
Reasons to conduct, 4
Six-month, advantage of, 19
Special, 20-22
Timing of, 11-22
Traditional. See Traditional reviews
Unscheduled, 21
World. See World reviews

Rewards
And the world review, 26
Frequency of, 19
Importance of, 4
Program, 119

Role-playing client situations, 4

S

Safeway Stores *v.* Retail Clerks, 130

Salary
Battles over, 120
Changes in, 40, 101, 118-120

Sample Employee Handbook Section on Employee Appraisals, 145

Scheduling, flexible, 7

Scores
Discrepancies in, 44
False, 33

Scoring
Trimmed mean, 44

Self-centeredness, 115
Self-confidence, lack of, 115
Self-evaluation forms, 31, 32, 38, 102, 114
Seminars, for staff training in world review evaluation, 28, 71
Service reminders, 35
Severance package, 127, 143
Sickness, employee, 48
Fraudulent use of sick leave, 132

"Silent sufferer," 118
Skill development, 7
Skills to emphasize, in a review, 37
Software programs, for employee evaluations, 147-148
Speaking badly, of practice or staff, 20
Special reviews
    When to conduct, 20
Standards, job, 43
    Variations on for the world review, 72-74
Stealing, 109, 132, 136, 141
Strengths, employee, 66-68, 93
    Determining how they maximize practice performance, 67
Strictness, 41-42. See also Errors, potential
Subjectivity, 38, 75
Suggestions, requesting from employees, 17
Summarization, of the review meeting, 113
Superstar employee, 40, 47, 72, 104-105
    Affirming work of, 105
Supervisors, 24, 26. See also Managers
Surgical abilities, 38
Sweating, by employee during review, 118

T

Tardiness, 92, 107
Team skills, as criteria for performance, 79-80, 115
    Does not avoid any aspect of job, 80
    Has a good attitude, 79
    Is cooperative, 80
Teamwork, 5, 6, 62
    And the world review, 25, 73
Technical skills, 37, 51-53
    Kennel assistants, 51
    Managers, 53
    Receptionists, 51
    Veterinarians, 52
    Veterinary technicians, 52
Technicians, 34, 50
    Accuracy, as criterion for evaluation, 58
    Efficiency, as criterion for evaluation, 58
    Goals for newly hired, 14
    Initiative, as criterion for evaluation, 64
    Knowledge base for, 54-55
    Medical skills required, 87
    Organizational skills needed for, 62
    Productivity in work, evaluation of, 56
    Skills to emphasize, 37
    Technical skills for, 52

Termination, 10, 17, 133
   Court cases related to, 123
   Retaliatory, 130
   Wrongful, 124
   Ways to avoid lawsuits for, 124
Theft. *See* Stealing
Thought collecting, before filling out review form, 35
360° *Feedback*, 25, 41
360-degree review, 25
Time cards, use of, 39
Timeliness
   Of employee, 35
   Of reviews, 11
Time periods, for accomplishment of goals, 13
Tip icons, 4, 5, 8, 9, 12, 13, 16, 18, 19, 24, 25, 33, 34, 40, 43, 47, 55, 84, 88, 92, 93, 99, 103, 104, 105, 108, 109, 110, 111, 114, 116, 119, 120, 125, 133, 137, 139, 140, 142
   Explanation of, 2
Toussaint v. Blue Cross and Blue Shield of Michigan, 129
Trade-offs, in performance standards, 74
Traditional Evaluation Form, 160-161
   Completed, 162-163
Traditional reviews, 23, 24, 31, 45, 47-70
   Advantages of, 24
   Determining overall performance for, 65-70
   Employee preparation for, 31
   Who they are most appropriate for, 47
Training, of reviewers in world review, 28, 42, 71
Trial period, 13, 17
   Extension of, 18
Turnover, employee, 6, 33
20/20 Insight Gold, 148

U

Ultrasound, 7
Unemployment insurance, 142
Upward review, 25. *See also* World reviews

V

Vendettas, personal, 33
Vendors
   As evaluators for the world review, 26, 32
Veterinarians, 50, 73, 76
   Accuracy, as criterion for evaluation, 59
   As contract employees, 126-127
   Efficiency, as criterion for evaluation, 59
   Goals for newly hired, 14
   Initiative, as criterion for evaluation, 64

    Knowledge base for, 55
    Organizational skills needed for, 62
    Productivity in work, evaluation of, 56
    Recently hired, 13
    Skills to emphasize, 37
    Special evaluation of, 86-87
    Technical skills for, 52
Veterinary assistants
    Skills to emphasize, 37
Violence, 132, 141
Vision, sharing of with employees, 7
"Volcano" reactions during the review, 117-118

W

Warning icons, 7, 9, 13, 17, 20, 25, 27, 29, 33, 41, 62, 65, 68, 72, 85, 93, 101, 105, 108, 109, 112, 114, 117, 118, 120, 124, 128, 129, 134. 142, 143
        Explanation of, 2
Warnings, 16, 33, 101
    Early, 19
    Verbal, 134-135
    Written, 10, 135-139
Weaknesses, 68, 93, 111
Week one, for new employees, 13-16
Weiner v. McGraw-Hill, 128
"Whistle-blower" protection, 127
Women
    And self-bias, 41
Work, substandard, 20
World Evaluation Form, 151-153
        Completed, 154-159
World reviews, 25-29, 45, 71-95
    Asking for comments during, 87-88
    Benefits of, 25-26
    Comments for, 94-95
    Cost of versus traditional review, 27, 28
    Employee preparation for, 31-32
    Importance of being specific in, 72
    Initial stages of, 71
    Overall numerical rating for, 92
    Performance criteria for, 77-87
    Rating scales for, 72
    Specific areas for evaluation, explanation of, 76-77
    Staff training for, 27-28
    Summarizing results of, 92-95
    Tallying results of, 88-92
    Used for career development, 26
    Variations on standards for, 72-74